WHEN YOUR CHILD NEEDS TESTING

WHEN YOUR CHILD NEEDS TESTING

. . .

WHAT PARENTS, TEACHERS, AND OTHER HELPERS NEED TO KNOW ABOUT PSYCHOLOGICAL TESTING

Milton F. Shore, Patrick J. Brice,
and Barbara G. Love

Foreword by William Van Ornum

A CROSSROAD BOOK
THE CROSSROAD PUBLISHING COMPANY
NEW YORK

1996

The Crossroad Publishing Company
370 Lexington Avenue, New York, NY 10017

Printed in the United States of America
Typesetting output: T{}EXSource, Houston

Library of Congress Cataloging-in-Publication Data

Shore, Milton F.
    When your child needs testing : what parents, teachers, and other
helpers need to know about psychological testing / Milton F. Shore,
Patrick J. Brice, and Barbara G. Love.
       p. cm.
    Includes bibliographical references and index.
    ISBN 0-8245-1192-1; 0-8245-1542-0 (pbk.)
    1. Psychological tests for children. 2. Psychometrics—Popular
works. I. Brice, Patrick J. II. Love, Barbara, G. III. Title.
BF722.S49 1992
155.4'028'7 — dc20   91-31652
                                               CIP

*We dedicate this book to all the parents
and those who work with and care for children.
We hope that their efforts to help children grow
and realize their potential are rewarded.*

Contents

Foreword

When Your Child Needs Testing is a powerful book. Milton Shore, Patrick Brice, and Barbara Love take the mystery out of psychological testing. They place the knowledge regarding testing children in its proper place: in the hands of parents. This is a theme throughout the book: "parents, not tests, are the ultimate decision makers about children." The book provides knowledge that dispels anxiety for parents who panic when they hear "Your child needs testing!" from a teacher or other professional.

This book is a small course on psychological testing. Everyone who works with children — teachers, administrators, social workers, speech therapists, and psychologists — will gain a better understanding of the topic. As a result, everyone will make better referrals. Readers will learn the wealth of expertise developed from a century of discovery in testing.

This book also challenges psychologists to conduct testing in the best possible manner. Informed clients provide quality assurance. The authors encourage parents to ask many questions, and help them ask the right ones.

What information can testing provide? *When Your Child*

Needs Testing explains when testing gives information that interviews cannot. Parents learn how to select a psychologist with the needed professional education and experience. Children become less anxious when grownups can explain reasons for testing to them — another focus of the book. To be an informed consumer of testing, parents need to learn the statistical properties of tests. A clear and readable presentation encourages readers to put aside math anxiety and learn about this aspect of testing.

Joseph Matarazzo defined testing as "emerging science based on art." Sometimes parents disagree with recommendations in a report, and they learn what to do next when this occurs.

Everyone involved with testing is mindful of confidentiality. A conflict occurs when parents desire to release helpful information to teachers but feel a need to keep other information to themselves in order to protect the family integrity. Parents and psychologists need to balance these different needs.

In this book there is a description of Public Law 94-142 and implications for testing. There are times when parents want an evaluation by someone not employed by the school district. Or, there may be a need when there is a serious emotional problem to find a psychologist with training and experience in child clinical psychology.

At the end of this book the reader will find a helpful bibliography, glossary, and appendix (which lists over 60 tests). Students of psychological testing will find this book an excellent resource in their training and professional development.

When Your Child Needs Testing comforts and empowers parents toward greater advocacy. Milton Shore, Patrick

Brice, and Barbara Love challenge psychologists to work at the highest levels of professionalism. Teachers, administrators, social workers, speech therapists, and others will gain a greater awareness of the wealth of information testing can provide. Written clearly and literately, *When Your Child Needs Testing* guides everyone in the grown-up world toward greater effectiveness in helping children. It is written by experts who understand testing from years of professional experience, and from the hearts and minds of children and parents.

William Van Ornum, Ph.D.
Marist College
Poughkeepsie, New York

Preface

The authors had many reasons for deciding to write this book for parents and professionals who work with children. First and foremost was the desire to be helpful to children. Our professional lives for the most part have focused on trying to facilitate growth and development of children. One of the ways to do this is to give parents as much support, encouragement, guidance, and reassurance as possible. We have found that this becomes particularly important when psychological testing of a child has been suggested. Although our professional backgrounds and work settings differ, as psychologists we all utilize psychological test procedures in many instances. In fact, it is rare nowadays to find someone whose life has not been touched by tests or test scores. Achievement, admission, even obtaining a driver's license involve testing procedures. It was our goal in this book to develop a guide that could be used to understand psychological testing procedures and to make the best use of them in decision making.

Our position, expressed throughout the work, is that parents are the people who make final decisions for their children. Psychological tests and measurement procedures, as part of an assessment process, only provide parents with information that can guide the decision making process. Test results alone cannot make decisions. At best, they help to ensure that decisions that are made benefit children. It has been our experience that literature that can serve as a guide to negotiating the entire psychological evaluation process has not been readily available to parents.

Parents routinely report that meetings to discuss results of psychological testing, particularly with school personnel, have been frightening, anxiety provoking, and at times overwhelming. The present book hopefully will aid parents in being more *active* participants, will help them to understand the process and terms used in the psychological assessment procedure, and thereby reduce the sense of helplessness often reported.

Many educators, social workers, or others who are involved with helping children may find this book helpful as an aid in explaining the process of assessment to parents or clients. While much of the focus in the book is on encouraging parents to be active, many of the same principles apply to others who work with children. Teachers, for example, know their students in a unique way and can be helpful in the evaluation by thinking about their students, how they behave in class and in school, what their skills appear to be and what their weaknesses are like. Teachers and others can also be active in the assessment process by talking with the psychologist, asking questions, and clarifying any points that are not clearly understood. Chapters 6 and 7 in particular may be useful for other professionals who wish to understand more of the principles in psychological testing. Psychological assessment is viewed here as the beginning of a helping process; it is the point where an understanding of the child often begins. This understanding may lead to a new awareness of normal development or to interventions (ranging from psychotherapy to school changes to development of new parenting techniques) that facilitate growth in children. The present work was not intended to be highly technical, though there are some parts that are more technical in an attempt to explain certain aspects of the testing process. In particular, the "numbers" or scores derived from testing are discussed in depth. However, the message throughout is that numbers may describe some skills in a child, but they do not define the child. An understanding of a child is not communicated through a table of scores, but through an interpretation of those scores in the context of other information about a child's life.

What follows is a description of a group of children of various ages for whom some sort of psychological testing has been suggested. These children will be discussed and referenced throughout the book as we attempt to illustrate testing as part of the assessment process, its values and limitations, and how parents can best negotiate the process. These children are fictionalized cases, though they are all realistic and represent the variety and kinds of referrals that are common. Our experience in psychological evaluations spans a wide continuum, from school-based assessments, to disabled children, to a general clinical population. This book has grown out of our experience with these children and their families.

Acknowledgments

We want to thank both Dr. Ronald B. Kurz and Dr. Frank R. Zieziula for their comments and reviews of earlier versions of this book. Their help was greatly appreciated.

WHEN YOUR CHILD
NEEDS TESTING

1

Your Child Should Be Tested

Tommy (case #1) is a white, eight-year-old boy. His mother had an extremely difficult pregnancy and spent many months on doctor-ordered bed rest, which was difficult because of her energetic personality. Tommy weighed a little over a pound when he was born almost two months prematurely, and had to remain in the hospital eight weeks before he could go home. Despite the stress on the family, both parents spent a great deal of time with him in the hospital, feeding him, holding him, and cuddling him in the nursery. As a baby, he was very quiet. He seemed to be slower in walking and talking than his ten-year-old brother. Tommy's parents noticed that although he was socially very adept, he was having problems in keeping up with the other children in math (he is in the second grade in a well-known private school). Pediatric examination was negative. His math teacher told both parents that she believes he is lazy and does not do his work. She feels that if he spent more time on his homework he would be able to do well. His parents feel (as does Tommy) that he is trying but easily gets confused, which causes him to cry when working on homework. He repeatedly says that math is too hard. After a discussion with the school principal it was agreed that Tommy should be referred for psychological testing.

Lisa (case #2) is a charming three-year-old whose parents (both white, middle-class individuals) are in their forties. This is the second marriage for both parents. After many years of trying to have a child (with numerous medical interventions), Lisa was born. Both her parents are hardworking computer scientists who feel strongly that they can combine careers with parenthood. They have worked diligently to divide the child care between themselves. Lisa is in day care from 8:30 to 4:30 every day. The day-care-center teacher has mentioned to the parents that Lisa seems different. Her speech seems delayed and she walks somewhat awkwardly compared to her classmates. Lisa also clings to her mother whenever she is in a new situation. Mother discussed these behaviors with Lisa's pediatrician and asked her what she thought. The pediatrician told her not to worry and that Lisa would outgrow those "problems." However, Lisa's parents wonder if there is some way to find out if she is developing properly. They have heard that psychological testing might be able to give them a better idea about how their daughter is doing.

Kelly (case #3) is a six-year-old Caucasian girl who has just started first grade, where she is a good student. Kelly is involved in many activities (choir, Girl Scouts, gymnastics) where she excels. Kelly's pediatrician has been following her for a number of months as she has begun to complain of stomachaches every morning. However, no physical basis for the pains has been found. Kelly's mother is a single parent. Her father, an alcoholic, rarely visits her. Over the past two weeks, Kelly has started wetting her bed and describing nightmares that are very frightening to her. Kelly's pediatrician, after reviewing the course of her treatment, suggested to her mother that she seek psychological testing to help understand Kelly's problems.

José (case #4) is ten years old and was born in a small town in El Salvador. He was sent to the United States three years ago by his parents, who remain in El Salvador. He is currently living with his aunt and five cousins in a three-room apartment. Everyone has been amazed at his remarkable command of English. He has many friends and the teachers in school are very fond of him. His family has told him not to mention to his teachers or anyone else that an uncle in El Salvador had been kidnapped from his home and his body was later found in a creek. José has great trouble concentrating in school. He is restless and sometimes jumps up from his seat when he hears a noise and begins to walk around the classroom. This has affected his performance in school. The teacher referred him to the school counselor. After meeting with the teacher and José, and talking with his aunt and uncle, the counselor suggested José be tested.

Jeremy (case #5) is a four-and-a-half-year-old black child. According to his mother, he has always been quite verbal. Family members who visit often say he is a genius and will undoubtedly be famous some day. Both parents, university professors, are worried that Jeremy may be bored in school. They feel he is gifted and talented. Although no one in his university-based nursery school had suggested testing, his parents brought him for testing because they wanted to know if Jeremy should be placed in a private school, should skip kindergarten, or should be placed in a program for gifted children when he started school. The results of the testing, to his parents' surprise, described Jeremy as bright, but immature. The psychologist recommended they not place him ahead or attempt to enroll him in any gifted or talented programs. Both parents, after getting over their surprise, felt that the evaluation was "unfair," since Jeremy was not feeling well that day and was just getting over the flu. They are considering getting a "second opinion."

Brad (case #6) is an eight-year-old black child whose parents divorced when his mother was three months pregnant. He has a long history of threatening other children and swearing at teachers for no apparent reason. Teachers have commented that Brad often seems "spaced out," even in the middle of a conversation. They will be talking to him and he stares at them with no comprehension in his eyes. At times he has been overheard to refer to himself as Michael. Grades at school have been quite variable. Mother, who has just turned twenty three, says there have been no problems at home (where she lives with her mother). She believes the school should be stricter, and that Brad is just playing games at school. However, at the teacher's request, Brad's mother has granted permission for the school psychologist to see him for an evaluation.

It has been known for years that Allison (case #7) was mentally retarded. An engaging, blond-haired child, she was born with Down's syndrome. Allison is now seven years old and has acquired a number of social skills. People enjoy her company as she is always cooperative and helpful. Many people think she is not as retarded as indicated by the IQ scores from earlier psychological testing. A neighbor has suggested that her parents have her reevaluated. When the parents checked with her school, the special education coordinator explained that Allison would be reevaluated every three years as part of the special education eligibility process.

The judge was concerned about Brian (case #8), a fifteen-year-old white male caught stealing a car. It was suspected that he was using drugs and alcohol. He has a history of verified sexual and physical abuse; Protective Services removed him from his home at age twelve and he has been in a foster home ever since. Brian talks back to all adults. He has been seeing a psychiatrist weekly for psychotherapy. The psychiatrist has been concerned about unusual homicidal and suicidal ideas Brian has discussed in recent sessions. Brian wants to drop out of school (he repeated first grade and is currently in the eighth grade). He has been described by teachers as out of control when he gets angry; any frustration causes him to strike out, and he has often been described as insensitive to others. He seems preoccupied with cars. Brian's psychiatrist recommended to the court that he have a psychological evaluation within a month to "determine what his needs are," particularly whether or not he should be placed in a protective treatment setting.

Julie (case #9), an eighteen-year-old Caucasian with cerebral palsy has always required extra time to do her work. Since she is graduating from high school this year she feels under pressure to decide whether to get a job or go to college. She wonders if she has the ability needed to do college work and if there are any colleges sensitive to her disability. She has no idea what she wants to do and is unclear about her own abilities and interests. After contacting her Vocational Rehabilitation Counselor and discussing her concerns with him, Julie decided to get psychological testing to help her decide what to do.

Edward (case #10) is a six-year-old Caucasian. Two weeks ago his dog, to whom he was very attached, was "put to sleep" because she was suffering with an untreatable disease. Edward does not want to go to sleep at night, has lost his appetite, and does not play with anyone. He says he still likes school, but he rarely smiles. His parents are worried that he is taking the loss too hard. They have not told him that when they go to bed they have cried since they too loved the dog dearly. They have promised him that they will take a trip to the pet shop and get another dog next week. However, his behavior hasn't changed and they are afraid that there might be a "psychological" problem.

As can be seen from the ten cases presented, there may be a number of reasons for suggesting psychological testing. Referrals for testing may come from many sources — doctors, friends, therapists, school personnel, courts, and others. Children of different ages, backgrounds, and situations may be referred. However, the common feature in each of these cases, as in all referrals for psychological testing, is that decisions have to be made regarding the identified problem.

When the problem is clearly delineated, the potential role of psychological testing in decision making is apparent. For example, Jeremy's (case #5) parents and Julie (case #9) are facing a dilemma regarding school choice. Developmental status is the major concern for

Lisa (case #2). Both Tommy's (case #1) and José's (case #4) teachers are requesting assistance in instructional planning. But commonality in presenting problems in these cases does not mean the role of psychological testing in decision making will be similar. In each of these cases the child's age, background, unique characteristics, and events of significance that might influence test results must be considered.

Frequently, referrals for psychological testing are based on nebulous or broad problem statements (e.g., "She doesn't have common sense."). In these cases, the specific problem and question need to be specified prior to testing. Consider two of the cases, both involving a teacher request for assistance in instructional decision making. For Tommy (case #1), academic problems are only apparent in math, with no other significant school- or home-based problems indicated. In contrast, José (case #4) is exhibiting a wide variety of behaviors that interfere in classroom performance. José's "trouble concentrating" and restlessness and Tommy's tears and confusion at homework time and negative attitude toward math explain poor school performance, yet offer no insight regarding intervention. Rather these descriptions lead to questions. Is José unable to concentrate because of his violent memories and worries about his family's well-being? Is he exhibiting signs of constitutional "hyperactivity"? Is Tommy's crying part of a long-standing pattern of getting attention or manipulating people? Is some event at home or with peers preventing him from focusing in school? For both José and Tommy, the potential underlying causes for the problem behaviors must be addressed in an effort to understand the problem and develop an effective intervention.

Problem specification and verification are complicated when multiple problem behaviors exist. For example, Kelly's (case #3) stomachaches, nightmares, and bed-wetting may all be reactions to a single underlying problem or event, or could be signs of a more general deficiency in stress-coping mechanisms. The judge in Brian's (case #8) case apparently recognizes the array of problem behaviors, beyond the theft for which Brian was arrested, as evidenced by a recommendation for psychological testing to assist in making a needs-based decision. To what extent have a history of academic failure, poor achievement motivation, low frustration tolerance, poor peer relationships, and alcohol and drug abuse contributed to Brian's current circumstances?

Sometimes there is consensus regarding problem specification, but problem severity must be verified prior to decision making. For example, Brian (case #8) is being treated in psychotherapy for behaviors related to a history of abuse and family disruption. However, Brian's psychiatrist is concerned that the severity of the disturbance exhibited is increasing. In Edward's case (case #10), his parents are concerned that his grief reaction may be more severe than normally expected for his age. Is he experiencing a normal grief reaction that has overtaken the whole family? Is he overreacting, or are his behaviors evidence of a general depressive tendency? In Brad's case (case #6), his mother and teacher agree that his behavior at school and his academic performance are problems; however, his mother sees "no problem at home." Is something going on inside Brad or is the severity of the problem a function of his environment? Could the difference in parent and teacher opinions reflect differences in expectations for Brad at home as compared to school?

Inconsistencies in available data may actually pose the presenting problem. Allison's (case #7) parents know she is mentally retarded, but are wondering if earlier test results reflect her current level of functioning? While that earlier testing may have assessed her intelligence, perhaps it did not take into account Allison's social adaptability. Has Allison's developmental rate been more rapid than predicted earlier? Answers to these questions have far-reaching implications for planning and decision making for her future.

Across these cases problem behaviors or situations were described. Psychological testing is frequently recommended to determine the reason(s) for behavior or to evaluate circumstances or situations to aid in decision making. All these cases introduce the concept of behavior as "multidetermined" and hint at the complexity involved in efforts to determine causes. Behavior is what can be observed — what someone does or says. Observed behaviors may reflect physical, cognitive, social, emotional, and/or personality problems or strengths. There may be many reasons for any given behavior, as well as a wide array of behaviors that may reflect the same general concern. Behavior changes as one grows. Behavior changes across situations or under different circumstances. The degree of complexity in human behavior and the variability in contexts within which people must operate underlie the major limitations associated with development and use of psychological tests.

If psychological testing is being considered as an aid in

decision making, care is warranted, particularly when it is for children who are unable to make their own choices. The following chapters are designed to answer questions frequently asked about psychological testing and offer suggestions to empower parents to make careful choices in seeking and using psychological testing:

- Why testing?
- How do I know if psychological testing is necessary?
- Who should do it?
- What will the experience be like?
- What kind of information will psychological testing give me?
- How can I use the information obtained?
- What are my rights and responsibilities?

The cases presented in chapter 1 will be used throughout this volume to illustrate various points in seeking answers to the questions posed. The hope is that information in this book will lead to more effective decision making if someone says, "Your child should be tested!"

2

Why Psychological Testing?

This is really silly; what does it show anyway?
— Fourteen-year-old girl halfway
through the testing session

WHY was psychological testing considered in each of the cases presented in chapter 1? To answer this question clearly, it is important to understand the unique characteristics of psychological tests, the context in which testing is done, and the value, as well as limitations, of psychological testing.

What Is a Psychological Test?

The word *testing* frequently elicits a number of associations. People think of school where tests are used to find out who has done the homework assignment and learned the material. If the material was learned, students passed; if not, they failed. This success/failure model arouses much anxiety among people being tested. Indeed, "test anxiety" is an experience many people have and one that has been studied extensively in psychology.

31

Another meaning of *testing* is associated with medical examinations. There are a number of medical tests, e.g., blood tests, that are used to determine whether or not a disease is present in the body. Traditional medical/laboratory tests are designed to discover physiological causes underlying symptoms. The results are independent of time and place. Thus, a high white blood cell count would strongly suggest a systemic infection, regardless of when or where the test was conducted. Electroencephalograms, CT scans, and magnetic resonance imaging techniques are tests of the neurological system that will yield the same results regardless of where they are given.

Psychological testing differs markedly from medical testing. In psychology, testing is a way of collecting information that helps us to understand psychological processes and behavior. Since behavior is multidetermined, i.e., it has biological, psychological, social, and cultural influences, it is important that psychological testing be distinguished from many other kinds of testing. And, unlike traditional medical/laboratory testing, the context can have significant effects. A test administered in a group setting, like a classroom where there are many students, may yield significantly different results than if it were administered individually in a psychologist's office. The result of a test given by someone who is liked by a child and where the child is relaxed differs from one where the child feels uncomfortable.

The very idea of measurement in psychology is abstract and complex. A physician can see or detect the physical presence of a tumor, aberrant blood cells, a virus, or bacteria with sophisticated laboratory tests and techniques. However, no one can see intelligence, memory, personality, or cognitive style. We can only deduce something about these characteristics from behavior. Therefore, measuring these psychological entities is more difficult, and as a result, less accurate than well-developed medical/laboratory tests. Because of these limits in psychological tests, multiple testing procedures and techniques are used as part of a process, usually referred to as psychological assessment.

What Is Psychological Assessment?

Psychological assessment is the procedure whereby a psychologist gathers information about a person in an attempt to answer some questions about behavior, emotions, personality, or cognitive (intellectual) abilities. An assessment typically encompasses several means or methods of collecting and distilling information. It is then up to the psychologist performing the assessment to integrate the information, develop and test hypotheses about the psychological process in question, and formulate answers to those questions.

The first source of information for a psychological assessment is gathered from existing documents, including files and records (e.g., court records, school records). For example, current testing should always be compared to previous testing to see what, if any, changes have occurred. School records are a picture of how the child is perceived by others in different situations. Records from other agencies assist in giving not only background data, but also in giving an understanding of where to begin and indicating differences in behavior across contexts. The psychologist doing the testing will evaluate the material for accuracy and will judge its relevance. The psychologist is alert to opinions, biases, and judgments made by others and will not have these influence findings in an inappropriate manner. This extremely important information cannot be obtained without written permission from parents.

A second technique for gathering information for assessments is observation. Commonly, the psychologist observes how the child performs on the tests and observes how the child is behaving in the waiting room. Still, the psychologist may want to supplement the testing with other observations (for instance at home or in the classroom). Observations are extremely important as a way of collecting information about specific problem behaviors. Observations permit a total picture of the natural context in which the problem behavior occurs over time. It is particularly useful when cooperation is a problem. It is possible to observe subtle changes and the impact of the situation as the behavior unfolds in interactions. The behavior is observed firsthand rather than reported. One difficulty with observations is that the behavior may not show at the time of the observation (people are often on their best behavior when being observed). The person's behavior at the time of the observation also may not be typical behavior. Observation also does not "reveal" the reason behind the particular behavior.

A third technique for gathering information for an assessment is the interview. A psychologist may use the interview to supplement testing. An interview is a communication between people to gather information. The interview may be an individual interview, a family or group interview, or a play interview with a child (play is the medium through which children communicate their thoughts and feelings). There is a common feature in each of these interview strategies — an opportunity to explore or proceed in a particular direction to gather more in-depth information. Through interviews, it is possible to gain anecdotal and observational data that helps put together a picture of the child and family in interactions.

The highly individualized aspect of the interview is its greatest asset. It gives people an opportunity to communicate in ways that are characteristic for them. The greatest asset of the interview, however, is also its disadvantage. Each interview is unique. It is practically impossible to compare one interview with another — the interviewers' styles differ, the material obtained differs, and there are often areas that are not explored. This may be because the client was unaware, unable, or unwilling to share certain things. Or, the interviewer may have felt that pursuing a certain area would not be helpful or would be impossible to follow up. A great deal of the material obtained in an interview depends on the skill and training of the interviewer. Gaining the cooperation of the interviewee and overcoming social graces that can cover significant areas of concern — and present the person in "the best light" — are issues that are difficult to deal with in an interview.

This brings us now to psychological testing as the last major means of collecting data. Psychological testing is a "picture" of behavior at a given point in time. It has unique advantages and contributes a great deal to the assessment process. There are five major values to psychological testing, which also help define it:

1. Psychological tests present a standard situation. All the individuals given the test are given the same instructions and the same questions. This is an attempt to make the experience similar for everyone so that the responses or reactions are not a result of different questions or cues, as is the case often in interviews. This contributes to the objectivity in testing that makes it valuable as part of assessment.

2. Efforts are made to objectively score the responses given. Testers are required to be trained in administration and scoring and often have their results checked to make sure they are scoring correctly.

3. A test is administered to a number of individuals who form a normative group. An individual child's answers (responses) are compared to the responses of that group. Thus, a more objective judgment can be made as to whether the person is or is not like others in certain ways.

4. Well-designed testing can answer some questions quickly: for example, whether or not someone is developmentally functioning significantly below his/her age mates.

5. It is almost impossible to fabricate on most tests (many tests have no right or wrong answers). This allows information to be obtained that might otherwise be unavailable or inaccurate.

There are several distinct advantages that testing provides when gathering information needed for a decision. For example, Lisa's (case #2) parents wonder about her development. At the age of three she seems to have delayed speech, trouble separating from her parents, and perhaps even motor coordination problems. However, many children grow and develop at different rates. Some children seem to have a lot to say at young ages, others develop language a little later. Yet, parents may not know the difference. So how do Lisa's parents get answers to their questions about her development? By giving a standardized test that allows comparisons of Lisa's scores in language, motor, and social skills to others of her age, a psychologist can begin to evaluate how much Lisa is like or different from her peers.

In a similar way, testing can be very helpful in Tommy's (case #1) situation. In the second grade, he is having problems in math. Interview and observation data can help to define his problems, see how he behaves in school and in math class, notice how his teacher responds to him and approaches him, and gather impressions and opinions. However, test data would be the critical factor in determining how far behind his peers Tommy is in math, plus what other sorts of weaknesses and strengths he may have that might suggest a true deficit for learning math.

Use of Tests in Assessment

Psychological tests have been used in a number of ways. Often they have been used in mechanical, routine ways to make decisions. Sometimes that is appropriate. For example, tests are given in a group setting to find out for whom further testing might be necessary or to find candidates for special programs or admission. This is called *screening*. Screening is usually completed with measures and techniques designed for group decisions. Thus, screening tests cannot and should not be used for determining what is underlying a behavior or as a substitute for a complete assessment. Their purpose is to eliminate those who do not require further consideration or attention or to select children for inclusion in certain programs.

With children, one might use screening tests to see if they are ready for certain workbooks in school, in need of tutoring or special help, or some other similar purpose. Screening offers an efficient way of using resources to identify a specific group needing attention. However, screening is a first step in certain types of decision making. The tests used are often brief and designed for group administration, thus will only provide crude "pictures" of the behaviors of concern. This will necessarily lead to some errors in decision making. Whenever an error is suspected, further testing is warranted.

Routine testing is common in some agencies where all clients take the same tests irrespective of the referral problem or issue. For example, in some correctional settings everyone gets an intelligence test; in another, an MMPI (an adult personality test). This mechanical testing procedure puts psychological testing on the same level as height, weight, and temperature measurements in a doctor's office. Psychological tests should be selected to answer certain questions and not used in a ritualistic manner. When used, it should be part of an assessment process or with a specific stated purpose in mind (e.g., screening). For some of the children described in chapter 1, psychological testing or assessment is not recommended, while for others it is. Testing children simply for the sake of testing has little merit.

In addition to screening, another reason for psychological testing is to determine if a *referral* for intervention is necessary. These tests can range from assessing for referral for a medication evaluation or review, to referrals for psychotherapy, to referrals for tutoring or a school change. Psychological tests can often provide information that will help in the assessment required to form the basis for a referral for intervention.

A frequent purpose for using tests in an assessment process is to help in making a *diagnosis*. The value of a diagnosis lies in being able to select appropriate treatment when necessary. José (case #4) may provide the clearest example where an accurate diagnosis of the ongoing psychological process is important. José shows symptoms that could be attributed to a post-traumatic stress disorder resulting from the traumas he witnessed in his home country of El Salvador. Those same symptoms, though, are also symptomatic of attention-deficit disorder, a disorder affecting many children. Psychological testing can be instrumental in diagnosing which of the two possible disorders underlies the observed behaviors. An accurate diagnosis is critical here since the intervention for post-traumatic stress disorder is quite different from the treatments normally recommended for attention-deficit disorder.

Another case where diagnosis becomes important is with young Brad (case #6). Some of the behaviors he has shown and others described may be suggestive of severe emotional disturbance. Calling himself another name, "spacing out" in the middle of a conversation, and the fighting and threatening are characteristics seen in pervasive developmental disorder. This is a disorder where children have poor understanding of reality and often lag behind in many areas of development. Yet, they may have a different underlying cause. They could be functional in nature, simply a strategy Brad has found to garner a great deal of adult attention. They could also result from a variety or combination of neurological difficulties such as an atypical seizure disorder. Psychological testing in this assessment can be helpful in discerning which of these factors is playing a major role.

Beyond screening, referral, and diagnosis, the most common use of psychological testing is in making plans for children. And the most common planning for children is educational. Psychological testing is usually seen as instrumental in placement decision making whenever any sort of special education options are being considered for children. These decisions, for example, could be whether a special school is necessary for a student, whether a self-contained classroom in a regular school will meet the needs in question, or whether resource room assistance will provide the required support.

While Jeremy (case #5) is young (four-and-a-half), a placement question has already been raised by his parents. From all they have gathered, their son is quite bright and may be gifted. If this is true, he may benefit from special classes or perhaps special schools to optimize his potential. Psychological testing will be a valuable aid to this process not only in determining whether Jeremy is "gifted," but also in providing insight into Jeremy's emotional maturity and perhaps his capacity to handle the pressures often experienced by gifted children.

Psychological testing can also be helpful to those planning instructional curricula. All children have different strengths and weaknesses in their learning styles. Knowing a child's learning style (e.g., experiential, visual, observer) helps the teacher/instructor plan the curriculum.

Placement decisions in education are not the only planning processes that take place. Testing may be requested to assess whether a child needs treatment of one sort or another. Brian (case #8) has been in treatment for some time. Yet, the recent behavior his therapist reports in therapy is worrisome and could be suggestive of suicide. While psychological testing cannot predict suicide with 100 percent accuracy, a full battery of testing with other data-collection methods can shed light on the kinds of despair Brian is feeling, the depths of that despair, as well as problem-solving approaches and coping strategies. In Brian's case, the testing can help in planning whether he can continue to be treated as an outpatient, or needs a more restricted/residential environment.

One more important use of psychological testing in assessments is evaluating change over time. Children in special education programs are required to have periodic reevaluations by psychologists to monitor changes in abilities. Because of the features of testing described earlier in this chapter, the availability of normative information, the standardized testing situation, and the objectivity of scoring in many tests, they provide a means by which to track change. It is certainly true that repeated testing or repeated exposure to the same test materials over a short time period biases the results. However, not all tests will be significantly influenced by practice effects. Furthermore, even tests influenced by practice can have that influence minimized by extending the time between testing.

Evaluating change in children through psychological testing is very common when children have experienced a head injury. There is often a predictable period of recovery for various kinds of injuries. It is possible, then, through observing changes in functioning on standardized psychological tests to track a child's recovery, or lack of recovery. Similarly, children who have experienced significant psychological trauma, such as abuse or neglect can be periodically reassessed to observe improvements in psychological functioning over time, as can children who receive special education services, whether in public or private schools or from a tutor.

These are some of the more common uses of psychological tests in assessments or evaluations. Obviously, children may be evaluated for some other purpose not described here. For example, judges may order children evaluated when there is a custody dispute in the courts or when consultation by a psychologist may be seen as useful. These reasons for referrals, while growing in number, are less frequent than the ones already described. Whereas psychological testing can be very helpful in many of these situations, it does have its limitations.

Limitations to Psychological Testing

Limited Predictability

As mentioned earlier, human behavior is multidetermined, with many factors interacting to influence behavior and functioning. Development does not occur in a vacuum. It takes place in a context that includes immediate family, community, and the larger society. A natural consequence of this is a limited ability to predict future behavior based on current psychological test data. This is especially true when a very young preschool child or infant is the subject in question. Psychological measures at young ages have little ability to predict later performance. This can be comforting to parents whose infant was assessed as having difficulties; there is hope that with help and an enriched environment the child can blossom. It should also serve as a caution to parents whose child was assessed as gifted or precocious in preschool.

Development also does not proceed in a step-by-step manner. There are peaks and valleys, periods of rapid change, and periods of consolidation. Each new period or stage in development brings new expectations, new environmental demands that hopefully match the newly emerging talents and abilities. Tests done at one point in time may not accurately predict how children will function at the next developmental level. What psychological testing can do is portray the child as he or she is at the given moment and provide insight regarding current underlying psychological processes. Based on these insights, psychologists can offer recommendations that will facilitate development, guide treatment or intervention, and address the referral question.

Overinterpretation of Scores

Some people may have a tendency to see tests as the "ultimate decision maker." No action is taken until the test results are seen, that is until the numbers are obtained. It is almost "number worship," or the tendency to attribute "power" to the numbers. Private schools sometimes set IQ cutoffs for entrance to the school. As a result, there may be a search for that IQ score by parents who want that school for their children. Strategies may be taught that will help children to achieve certain scores ("numbers") on entrance exams or on achievement tests. Psychological tests are seen as useful only in that they may provide numbers needed as entry tickets for the most sought after programs. This is a use of psychological testing that we do not support or encourage. It places minimal emphasis on what is actually best for the child, on what the child is ready to handle, and major emphasis on competition and achievement. Often this happens at an age where children are not ready emotionally to handle that kind of competition.

Parents, not psychological tests, are the ultimate decision makers regarding children. Psychological test data can be useful and hopefully will help professionals make useful and appropriate recommendations using other information as well; thus, parents get help making difficult decisions about their children. In the end, it is the psychologist, not the test data, and the parents, not the test data, who after interpretation, will use the material for the benefit of the child. When the numbers are taken out of the context of the testing and the child's life, they lose meaning. For example, Jeremy (case #5) may be intellectually gifted. Yet, other factors such as social and emotional maturity may suggest that he not be enrolled in a gifted program.

We will be stressing throughout this book that psychological tests must be interpreted to be useful. Numbers do not stand by themselves. In the same way that development does not occur in a vacuum, tests do not answer questions by themselves. Only when well-trained professionals integrate the data from tests with observations, interviews, etc., can appropriate opinions be offered and recommendations made.

Limited Comparison Groups

Some of the features of tests that make them valuable are also drawbacks. The fact that standardized tests have normative data allows comparisons of children with similar-aged peers as a way to gauge development and progress. *Normative data* refers to the scores obtained from the comparison group that will serve as the standard for judging performance. Unfortunately, normative data is sometimes limited when special populations are considered. For example, few measures of intelligence have included children who are deaf or hard-of-hearing in their normative sample. Therefore, when evaluating a deaf child, it is much harder to find a test that was developed using an appropriate comparison group. The same problem is true with other special populations, as well as ethnic or racial minorities. When the group of children upon which test norms were established does not include a cultural subgroup, that test cannot be used in the same way with children from that particular subgroup.

Inappropriate Uses

Tests are constructed to measure specific traits or characteristics (e.g., intelligence, personality, etc.). They are constructed with certain assumptions in mind. For example, since it is assumed that boys and girls are intellectually equal, IQ tests have been constructed so that those items that showed marked differences between the sexes were eliminated. A test measuring knowledge of math facts cannot be used as a measure of creativity or artistic ability. A test set up to measure personality cannot be used to assess cognitive or intellectual abilities. This is because the tests were constructed to focus on issues related to intelligence, knowledge of math facts, or personality, and to minimize the focus on other characteristics. Because of this, tests cannot and should not be used to assess other characteristics not built into the design of the measure.

This limitation is included because it does happen that psychological tests developed for one purpose have been used for something very different. Such uses are inappropriate. If there is need for measurement of a particular characteristic, then a procedure for measuring that characteristic should be used or developed.

Limits in Generalization

Test data are also time limited. As a "snapshot" of behavior, they lack the dynamic qualities that define the transactions between people. Generalizing from the results of a single, brief testing session to a child's life must be done with great caution and care. A long list of factors can color test results, such as the attitude of the child toward the testing, the child's health on the day of the testing, whether he or she remembered to bring his or her glasses (and whether the examiner knew glasses were even used!), and even the weather can influence this snapshot of behavior. Test interpretation, therefore, is always done from a cautious stance with a vigilant approach that seeks to encompass and explain behavior within context(s).

The thoroughness of the evaluation also has an impact on generalizability. When the evaluation is a simple screening, with one test given, there is very limited generalization. In contrast, when the test is part of a complete battery of a carefully selected group of tests and assessment procedures, psychologists can have more faith in how the results generalize to the child's life.

Psychological testing is a useful and effective way of collecting information about a child. This information, when supplemented with facts, impressions, and descriptions from other sources, leads the psychologist to form an opinion regarding the referral question. The psychologist also evaluates the confidence he or she has in the data and the results, and how accurately they characterize the child.

If psychological testing is appropriate for a child, the next question becomes, "How do I start?" What do I do to get the best possible evaluation for my child or my client?

3

How Do I Begin?

What do you think about me?
— Six-year-old boy talking to his father

TOMMY'S (case #1) parents were upset with his teacher for suggesting that he is "lazy" and requested a conference with the principal because they felt that many of his problems in math were the result of her teaching style. They were surprised (and angry) to find that the principal also inferred that the problem may be Tommy, not the teacher, since psychological testing was recommended by the principal.

Kelly's (case #3) mother goes home and cries after the pediatrician suggests psychological testing to help understand the reasons for Kelly's bed-wetting, nightmares, and somatic complaints. She feels that this recommendation either "indicts" her as a "bad mother" (even though she knows she has tried), or implies that her daughter has a mental problem. Kelly's mother feels frightened and threatened.

Allison's (case #7) parents felt they had accepted her mental retardation. The suggestion by a neighbor that a psychological reevaluation could reveal more potential has led them to feel "cautiously optimistic." However, they also remember how difficult it was to adjust to the results of the first evaluation. They wonder if professionals really know what they are talking about and wish they were not feeling like they were on a "roller coaster."

Jeremy's (case #5) parents are considering psychological testing based on their own views of Jeremy as "exceptional." However, they are somewhat anxious that results of psychological testing may not confirm their view of Jeremy. More and more they find that they have a great deal invested in their son's success.

These parents are experiencing normal emotional reactions of fear, anxiety, anger, and hope in response to someone's suggesting an evaluation of their child. Whether the suggestion for testing is to address a problem as in Kelly's and Tommy's situations, or is indicated as a means of validating a child's strengths, as in Allison's and Jeremy's cases, an emotional reaction should be expected. As the "ultimate decision makers" for their children, these parents do not have to respond to the recommendations made for psychological testing. They may choose to ignore the possibility of a problem. They may even choose to deny their feelings. Or they may ask themselves questions about their children and themselves, some of which may be uncomfortable.

Parents' emotional reactions to the possibility of psychological testing of their child may, in part, reflect erroneous assumptions about the nature of psychological testing. Parents may assume that testing will "tell" them about their child; or lead to decisions and choices that are incongruous with their hopes, dreams, and ideals for their child; or reveal their inadequacies as parents.

They may think that there is a "perfect" way to parent and that psychological testing reveals specific "errors" in parenting.

Parents often fail to realize (and it bears repeating) that testing is only a "snapshot" of their child, completed in a setting to which the child may never return while, as parents, they are privy to a dynamic picture of their child; or, to continue the analogy, a "comprehensive videotape" that reveals a view of the child from birth, across different situations or contexts. If such a "video" really existed, parents would simply take it to a psychologist for review as part of the evaluation. But no parent has such a video. Rather, they have records, memories, impressions, and, most important, feelings about their child that put them in the unique position of knowing their child as a "whole" — not just as a student, patient, playmate, or relative. This perspective is a critical component in gaining an understanding of the child. It is this dynamic view of the "whole child" that proves invaluable in guiding the psychological assessment process. But how does a parent become an active participant in the assessment process instead of a passive consumer of a professional service?

The starting place for any parent considering psychological testing is to think about the child. While as parents we may often talk about and think about what our children are like, organizing those thoughts can be very helpful. Furthermore, sitting down and actually thinking about our children can help to focus us on the issues and concerns that are most important. It can also force us to look at aspects of a child's life that we might otherwise overlook. How, then, can we organize our thoughts in preparation for meeting with a psychologist to discuss an evaluation?

In all ten cases from chapter 1, psychological testing was suggested by someone to aid in decision making regarding the child. With the exception of a few situations, the cases included problem statements that led to questions that should be addressed in order to clearly specify and verify the nature of the problem(s). But, when parents (or anyone) ask one question about the identified problem(s), it can naturally lead to other questions, as in the following examples:

> Is Edward (case #10) overreacting, or is he experiencing a normal grief reaction that has overtaken the whole family? Is he blaming his parents for what happened to the family pet? Or are all of his behaviors a sign of some other kind of emotional disturbance?

> Did Brian (case #8) steal the car simply for attention from someone? Is he antisocial and uncontrolled or was he trying to find someone who would stop him from doing something worse?

> Are Kelly's (case #3) stomachaches a reaction to some specific concern or worry? Do they tend to happen before big events at school or in extracurricular activities? Are they at all related to contacts with her estranged father? What does she get in terms of reaction from the family when she is suffering?

This is actually the first phase of psychological assessment. When parents begin thinking and asking themselves questions about their children, they are taking an active stance in the process. Thinking about what the particular child is like in relation to other children, as a family member, as a student, as a son or daughter begins to organize information. What follows is a beginning — a general guide for parents in asking questions, gathering information, and organizing so they can be actively involved in the psychological assessment process.

Asking Questions

Parents are accustomed to talking about their children with other people. They discuss growth, behavior, and health with the pediatrician; preschool teachers were ready to answer questions about parent-child separation, early social interactions, and preschool skill development. Teachers and principals have answered questions about admissions or achievement test results and classroom performance in terms of academic progress and behavior. Family members, friends, or neighbors may have eagerly shared their views when concerns or questions were voiced. Thus, over the years parents amass considerable information — often unsolicited — about their children from a variety of individuals.

The "making of a videotape" of a child will be a process of thinking about a child and answering questions about him or her. When parents begin asking themselves questions about their child, they soon begin to realize that while they don't have all the answers, they do have many. They know how their child has changed over the years; they know what the child meant to them when he or she was born; they know their child's habits, likes, and dislikes. Parents may also begin to realize that their child's world has broadened over the years to include people and places they may not know well or to which they are not privy (particularly with teenagers). To make the video comprehensive, there must be observations, or descriptions from many sources.

Questions Parents Can Address

To start organizing thoughts about children, parents can think of all the questions they have already answered. From birth, a variety of records are established for children where parents provide the information. Parents answer many types of questions: questions about family medical and social history, and pregnancy (typically for the hospital upon admission for childbirth); questions about birth and development for the pediatrician or family physician; and questions about immunizations and medical history for the school. Parents are often asked to provide facts about their children and their family.

Unfortunately, across the cases in chapter 1, it becomes readily apparent that *factual* information, from a historical perspective and a description of current problem behaviors is insufficient to address the complex problem(s) posed. Facts and descriptions fail to capture the "dynamic" qualities of a child when placed in different situations or under different kinds of demands. To gather this information, parents must ask questions that will help characterize their child. They must also think about the environments or contexts in which the child lives and to which the child must adapt.

It is important for parents to think about the different situations in which their children live, such as day care, school, and home. Parents can answer many questions about the family structure and home. For example, parents can define the family. This task may not be a simple one, as many children are involved in multiple family units as a result of custody arrangements in divorce. In many families, extended family members take an active role in child rearing. As a result, parents need to think about the child in each "family" unit identified for the child. Who lives in the home? What is a typical day like, from rising to bedtime? What changes has the family undergone during the child's lifetime? What significant stressors has the family had to face? Are there significant family members who live outside the home who play a role in the child's life, such as grandparents? How do family members differ in temperament and personality characteristics? How do different family members perceive and relate to the child?

To characterize a child, it is essential to include descriptive information about physical, cognitive (intellectual), temperamental, personality, social, and attitudinal behaviors features. Sample questions include:

How would I describe my child's appearance?

Does my child have any sensory impairments or physical limitations?

Is my child usually a leader or a follower?

What special abilities does my child exhibit?

Are there any type of activities my child customarily avoids?

Is my child focused or distractible, persistent or apathetic, reflective or impulsive?

Does my child prefer to be alone or with other children?

What does my child do best?

What is my child's temperament like? Is my child easy, slow or difficult in responding to changes or demands?

What kind of diet does he or she prefer?

What times of day are better and worse for my child?

Is my child moody or pretty consistent?

What kinds of television shows are preferred?

How does my child react when physically sick?

The specific information needed for an evaluation will vary and depend on the case and the referral question. Julie's (case #9) evaluation for career planning would not need this level of background or description. To address the referral questions for Brad (case #6) or Brian (case #8) the psychologist would require more information. Also, it is not necessarily suggested that parents write out lengthy answers to these kinds of questions on paper and bring them to the psychologist. Often the necessary information will be obtained by the psychologist from the referral source (if other than the parents). However, this is a first step in thinking about a child in an effort to understand him or her and to be prepared for an interview. Thinking in this way about a child can often lead to better recall of previous situations or facts that may prove useful.

Let's return to the cases from chapter 1 to see what types of questions parents of these children could ask. Edward's (case #10) parents may ask themselves if he has seemed sadder than their other children or if he has, generally, overreacted emotionally to most events at home. Kelly's (case #3) mother may keep a calendar to track the occurrences of bed-wetting, nightmares, and stomachaches, along with her daily activities and any special events or family circumstances because she wonders if there is some reactive pattern. Tommy's (case #1) parents can think about his reaction to school in general. Has he liked his teachers? Has he talked about his friends in positive ways? What was arithmetic like in first grade for Tommy? Were there any signs of problems there? How has he handled problems in the past? Has he always cried easily about things?

Questions Parents Should Ask Others

As children grow older, they spend increasing amounts of time outside the home. Today, many young children are in day care from infancy, as both parents may be employed. Comprehensive care of children includes numerous helpers — physicians, nurses, teachers, sitters. Thus, many other adults are involved in the lives of children. In thinking about a child, parents must consider these other sources of information.

Most parents are aware of the procedures and their legal rights with regard to obtaining medical and school records that contain factual data. However, gathering information about the "dynamic" characteristics of their child and the contexts within which the child is expected to function will usually require talking with others.

Next to home, school or day care may be the place where children spend most of their time. Each day care or school situation a child has experienced should be thought of with regards to physical characteristics, location, staff characteristics, peer exposure, and type of program provided. Reasons for change in school or day care center should also be considered. Qualitative or narrative descriptions of a child by teachers and other staff who work with a child may afford valuable insights, particularly when academic problems are of primary concern. This is why psychologists typically ask for written permission to contact schools and day care programs.

Social contexts for a child may be in the community, at school, family activities, or through pursuit of interests or enrichment, as in soccer, dance lessons, or theater. The family's neighborhood may be the primary source of enduring friendships for some children. However, children's social relationships may develop through other means. Family activities such as church involvement, social clubs, or social gatherings with other families may provide consistent exposure to other children. As neighborhood schools are not necessarily the norm for many children, school-based friendships may be difficult to maintain without parent involvement. The social nature of enrichment activities provided may be discerned by gathering information about opportunities for unstructured social interactions, a description of other children involved, location, and other identifying information. Generally, opportunities for development of social interests and friendships should be reviewed carefully.

Organizing Information in Contexts

Let's return to Edward (case #10) to consider how his parents might approach this task of "characterizing" him, in their efforts to create a "video." Edward's parents may wish to look at the family context and how various family members view him now, as well as in the past. Often family members' views of situations and members are not congruent. Discussion of the situation individually with various family members may allow recognition of differences in perception, which could be helpful in understanding and approaching a problem.

Having information about various school programs, such as brochures, reports, newspaper articles, or descriptions from administrators can be useful to compile and perhaps bring in to these evaluations. Equally important, though, is the impression the parents have of the program, their satisfaction or dissatisfaction, and their expectations. This, coupled with the reasoning and thought that went into the selection process is very important information.

The dynamic view of the child must come from all of the individuals involved with the child. His parents might ask for feedback from each of Edward's teachers to learn how he is behaving in school. While his parents may have seen his sadness at home, without talking with teachers they cannot know how much of his life it seems to pervade. Adults involved with Edward in other social or competitive activities (for example, his Little League coach, swimming teacher, family friends, or parents of his peers) might be asked to describe him as well.

What Edward's parents will probably find is that he behaves differently across contexts and with different people within many contexts. For example, he is described as an excellent young athlete for a six-year-old by both his swimming and baseball coaches, but he consistently performs at a "competitive" level only in swimming. At school, Edward is described as a good student by his art teacher, where his projects are well done. Yet, in more academic subjects such as reading or arithmetic, Edward has recently been described as inattentive, poorly organized, and distractible. At home, Edward's parents see him differently. His father recently began placing more demands on him regarding household chores. For example, Edward is expected to put his clothes away, take out the trash, and help clear the table. He often forgets some of these chores and requires a reminder. In contrast, his mother sees him as compliant. However, Edward's father feels that as Edward is the last of the children left at home, his mother has a tendency to "baby" him.

In addition to describing Edward's behavior across different contexts and with different individuals, his parents have also put together a history, where they have combined family, school, and medical information along with their impressions and those of others who have known Edward since birth. What they have learned is that Edward has frequently been described by others as being sensitive, and sometimes as moody. He is also recognized as skilled athletically and in activities depending on hand-eye coordination such as puzzles, video games, or model construction. Edward avoids verbal games and extended conversations. He has generally been described as a physically attractive and likable child. He has sustained relationships with peers, is usually included in activities at school, but becomes shy when it is his turn to lead an activity. He is helpful when he sees someone in need.

In reviewing the "video," Edward's parents now wonder if his current behavior is "reasonable," given the recent loss of the family pet, although some of the descriptions of him over the years seem consistent with a view of him as a shy and perhaps very sensitive young lad. This question of reasonableness is not one they can answer. Such a question may be addressed through a formal consultation with a psychologist, which may be sought with or without Edward's direct participation. At this point, all information gleaned through the questioning phase may be brought to the psychologist who might assist in the decision-making process regarding psychological testing—whether it is necessary and, if so, specifically what focus should the testing take.

How Much Should I Share?

One piece of information has not been directly addressed by Edward's parents. They have grown increasingly estranged since his two older siblings left home for college last fall. In recent months they have discussed a formal separation, but not directly in front of or with Edward.

This piece of information may or may not be the key to the problems Edward is experiencing. But there is no doubt that it is critical in attempting to put together a view of Edward as a "whole child," attempting to cope with many changes simultaneously. Parents must weigh the potential value with regard to problem resolution for their child and their need to protect the family integrity.

Often parents may not wish to share personal information with a school, particularly if not openly discussed with family members. This is understandable. However, if a child's school performance is affected by a family circumstance, the school may need some assistance in determining how to respond. A psychologist will maintain family confidentiality regarding such information (See chapter 9), but these arrangements should be made clear.

Beyond the Obvious Answers

Often parents may focus on the current description of a problem, avoiding asking historical and contextually based questions. Sometimes thinking about the past is not easy for people, especially when there has been difficulty in relationships or traumas in the family. A focus on the "here and now" also may be due to the severity or distress associated with the current problem. Take Kelly's case (#3), for example. Appropriately, Kelly's mother first focused on the most obvious aspects of the problem. The pediatrician may have asked Kelly's mother numerous questions about her diet, elimination, and sleep habits over the course of several months in an effort to explain recurring stomachaches. Specific medical tests were probably completed, as the symptoms deemed appropriate. Through a relatively structured series of questions and tests, all related to Kelly's physical well-being, the pediatrician could not find a physical basis for the stomachaches. It was then that psychological testing was suggested. Given the history of divorce, alcoholism, and estrangement from Kelly's father, asking questions and organizing information across contexts may be a painful process for Kelly's mother. The psychological assessment of Kelly may need to proceed in a manner that offers support for both Kelly and her mother at each step.

Regardless of the approach, a parent should ask questions as they arise at each step of the evaluation. No question is trivial. Any information parents have regarding who their child is may prove helpful. Enlisting the aid of others involved with a child is expected — teachers, physicians, or mental health professionals are trained to assist parents by sharing their information through formal and informal reports. Seeking assistance in organizing the information through psychological consultation does not mean that parents will not have input. Rather, the parents will want to maintain an active, participatory stance, reflecting and reviewing information for accuracy and consistency with their view of their child as a "whole."

4

Who Should Do It?

Will I get a shot from this doctor?
— Five-year-old girl being tested by a psychologist
in the outpatient psychiatry department of a hospital

SINCE important decisions will be made on the basis of the psychological evaluation, part of which may include psychological testing, it is essential that the testing be done by someone with adequate training and experience. As has been said, the quality of the results of psychological testing depends on a number of factors, not the least of which is the relationship between the examiner and the child. Experience in testing adults is not adequate preparation for testing children and adolescents. An understanding of child development and specialized training are necessary. How does a parent, therefore, select the most appropriate person to test their child?

Often a friend, relative, pediatrician, or school person will recommend someone. You, as a parent, however, have the right to inquire about the examiner's background and experience. What follows is some general information that you can use to check out qualifications.

There are many different types of psychologists; some have been trained to administer, interpret, and make appropriate recommendations based on the results of psychological testing. Others have less training in assessment and focus on different activities, such as group therapy or consulting. Psychologists, according to the American Psychological Association, should have a doctoral degree in psychology from an accredited university. In order to protect the public all fifty states and the District of Columbia regulate by law the practice of psychology. This is done either through: (1) certification or (2) licensure. Certification regulates the title of psychology, while licensure laws regulate the activities and functions that constitute the practice of psychology. To be licensed or certified the psychologist must meet certain training requirements and pass a national licensing examination. Sixteen states (Alaska, Arkansas, California, Iowa, Kentucky, Maine, Michigan, Minnesota, Missouri, New Hampshire, North Carolina, Oregon, Tennessee, Texas, Vermont, and Washington) have statutory recognition of some psychological practice at a master's degree level. These are usually called "psychological assistants" or "psychological associates" and ordinarily function under the supervision of a licensed or certified psychologist qualified for independent and unsupervised practice (Iowa, Minnesota, Missouri, West Virginia, and Pennsylvania license at a masters level for independent practice in psychology).

School psychologists not trained to the doctoral level are often certified for service within educational settings by state departments of education or the National Association of School Psychologists. To obtain national certification the school psychologist must complete a certain number of postmaster's credit hours, a twelve-hundred-hour supervised internship in school psychology (of which six-hundred hours must be in a school setting), be licensed or certified by their state department of education, and obtain a passing score on the National School Psychology examination. Unless they reside in a state that licenses nondoctoral psychologists for independent practice, however, these school psychologists *may* be limited to practice in school settings or under the supervision of a psychologist licensed for independent practice.

Licensure, however, is generic and does not ensure that the psychologist has had adequate training in diagnostic and treatment work (health service). Some states license for *any* professional psychological practice, including teaching and research. Therefore, in 1975, the Council for the National Register of Health Service Providers in Psychology was established. This organization evaluates the training and experience of psychologists who apply (qualifications are a doctoral degree in psychology, an internship in a service setting, postdoctoral supervised experience, and licensure by the state). There are a number of qualified psychologists who choose not to belong to the Register. However, there are now some sixteen-thousand psychologists who are listed in the Register's directory as having met the minimal standards of health service training.

Neither licensure nor the listing in the National Register directory guarantees competence. The closest the field of psychology comes to evaluating the competence of a psychologist is the peer review examination for the Diplomate of the American Board of Professional Psychology (ABPP). A psychologist may choose to take the examination for the diplomate after five years of post-doctoral experience. The examination consists of the observation and evaluation of a candidate's clinical skills by three senior diplomates. Diplomate examinations are currently being given in clinical psychology, counseling psychology, family psychology, industrial/organizational psychology, school psychology, clinical neuropsychology, and forensic psychology. The Board publishes a listing of all diplomates. There are currently some three thousand diplomates in the United States.

It must be emphasized here that licensure, listing in the National Register, and even earning a diplomate from the American Board of Professional Psychology does not *guarantee* that a particular psychologist has training and competence in psychological testing. Further, it does not guarantee that the psychologist has expertise in testing children, or is up to date with the latest advances in the field. Parents must still be willing to ask a psychologist specific questions about his or her training and experience.

In addition to specialized training necessary to evaluate children adequately, a number of subspecialties have arisen in child testing. Infant testing requires additional training. Neuropsychology has become a subspecialty with specially devised tests used to determine the integrity of the child's nervous system as well as to assess a wide variety of brain functions. Thorough psychological testing for learning disabilities requires the integration of psychological and educational testing techniques. This integration is to verify that learning problems are due to difficulties processing information, and not emotional or psychological issues. At times, "psychoeducational" evaluations are done by professionals with training in the assessment of learning styles and problems. While these professionals may be well trained, only licensed psychologists or those working under their direct supervision are legally able to conduct "psychological" evaluations. At times, further assessment beyond a psychoeducational evaluation may be necessary to determine whether emotional factors may be affecting school performance.

According to the code of ethics of the American Psychological Association, psychologists must only function in areas of their training and competence. When they receive referrals outside their areas of expertise, psychologists must ethically refer to someone more appropriately trained. You have the right to inquire about a psychologist's training.

You also have to recognize that even if you have chosen a competent psychologist for testing your child, the test situation is a very personal one, and requires that you and your child be comfortable. Thus, even after checking out all aspects and qualifications you should trust your intuition. Take the time to talk with the psychologist over the phone, or meet him or her before starting. Be willing to ask questions about years of experience, ages of children usually tested, training in the type of evaluation you are seeking, typical problems that he or she sees in the practice, percentage of practice devoted to a specialty area, years licensed, fees, payment procedures, where the evaluation will take place, what is typically done in such an assessment, whether interviews are done with other people if needed (assuming you give written permission), whether visits can be made to school if necessary. In addition, ask about issues related to your specific needs and the needs of your child. Even in a public school setting where the evaluation is at no direct cost to you, you have the right to ask questions of the person who will be seeing your child.

Most important is to inquire about adaptation to any special needs your child might have. For example, if your child is hearing impaired, the psychologist should be told and you should know that he or she has the training and background in the psychosocial and cultural aspects of deafness, as well as the necessary communication skills. If your child is bilingual and/or bicultural (as José – case #4), what knowledge does the psychologist have of the other culture and language? If there are physical challenges (as with Julie's – case #9 – cerebral palsy), does the psychologist have the necessary equipment, tests, and facilities to do a proper evaluation? A psychologist should also be told if there are any significant events occurring in the child's life.

The amount of time necessary to do a thorough evaluation varies a great deal. You may want to inquire about the psychologist's availability. Flexibility is particularly important when a child is resistant to testing. In such cases additional sessions may be necessary. Indeed, the psychologist may choose to test over a period of time in order to evaluate changes that might be taking place. Where problems are complicated the process of testing may be slower since it is essential that there be adequate rapport between the child and the examiner in order to obtain valid results. You may want to inquire regarding what kind of report will be given and when the results and report will be available.

In independent evaluations, it is recommended that issues regarding billing and fees be clarified. Parents should expect to be told whether the psychologist bills at an hourly rate, what that rate is, and what is included in that rate. For example, is travel time to a school included, is he or she billed for the time it takes to score a report, for the time a psychologist talks with others, etc.? Some psychologists have a flat rate they charge for a standard evaluation, with additional charges assessed if further testing is deemed necessary or requested in the beginning. Further, if a psychologist will be requested to attend staff meetings at schools or other agencies, there will oftentimes be a charge for that. All of these sorts of charges should be clarified. It should also be mentioned that various insurance companies handle reimbursements for psychological testing in different ways. Some reimburse for the entire service (after the deductible, of course), others will only reimburse if a physician or psychiatrist has recommended it in writing, and still others will not pay for evaluations at all, even though they may pay for therapy. It is important that you check with your own insurance representative about your policy's provisions.

As can be seen, there are a great many issues to consider when choosing or working with a psychologist. These vary from issues of training and credentialing to specific service experiences, to issues of comfort and sensitivity. It is impossible to say that one factor outweighs another, but it is important that you take an active role in the process. Doing everything you can to ensure that any assessment done is thoughtful, thorough, and accurate is one way of coping with a difficult and often trying situation.

5

What Should a Child be Told?

Will this show if I'm crazy?
— Ten-year-old boy in an outpatient clinic

PSYCHOLOGICAL testing has always had an aura of magic. What strange things will be discovered? What recommendations will be made? It arouses concerns and discomfort. There is fear that it will reflect on parenting skills or that the child may be hurt. Embarrassment, shame, and anger all come into play and make it difficult for a parent to prepare a child for testing. Thus, out of helplessness and suspicion, children have been told that they are going to a doctor (unspecified), to a play person, to a teacher, and in one case to the zoo!

Parents should feel free to ask the psychologist doing the testing what he or she would recommend telling the child. However, the basic principle regarding preparation is being honest in a way that can be helpful and at the same time be at a level that can be understood by the child. Thus, a child who is acting up can be told that there are reasons why someone keeps getting into trouble and that testing will help by finding out the reasons. If a child is frightened, saying that as a parent you are concerned that he or she is so scared and unhappy and we all are trying to find out why so we can be helpful. If a child is to be tested academically we can say that we are trying to find the best place for him or her so he or she can do well in school and enjoy learning.

Kelly (case #3) is showing signs that are very disturbing to parents and children, stomachaches, bed-wetting, and nightmares. Her mother, in preparing her for the testing could say something like the following: "Dr. Jones (the pediatrician) and I have talked about what might be making your stomach hurt every morning. She thinks we should see Dr. Smith (the psychologist). Dr. Smith will try to help us figure out what is making your stomach hurt so much. He will also help us try to figure out what's making it hard for you at night time with the scary dreams you've been having."

It is important not to say that the doctor will find out why the child is "bad" or why the child "doesn't listen." By stressing the negative things that the child is doing (and thereby being critical), a parent can set the child up to be the "bad guy" when the child gets to the evaluation. He or she will expect the psychologist to be on their parents' side and will not envision the evaluation as anything positive. Along with this, it is equally important to explain to children that they are not being evaluated because they are "crazy." Some children may reason like this: "Psych people deal with the crazies or the goof-offs. I am going to see a shrink. I must be crazy."

The help, it has to be made clear, is through the child talking to a "talking and playing doctor," not a doctor who will stick them with needles or do physical examinations. The information gathered by the doctor will then be kept in confidence unless there is reason to share it (for example, anything that might physically hurt somebody). The message is to share feelings and information, a message that is extremely important to convey. Also mentioned can be some of the techniques — there might be drawings, stories, questions, puzzles, or other activities (focusing on those areas that the child might find enjoyable). Although the description may sound like play, the language used needs to stress the help that will result from understanding the problem.

Whenever talking to children about important topics, it is very useful to get their current understanding of an issue first. Even something as different or unique as being evaluated by a psychologist can conjure up images in a child's mind. Asking a child what he or she thinks a psychologist does, or what a testing session might be like can give clues to parents as to how to talk to children. More children have seen psychologists now than when today's parents were children themselves. Tommy (case #1) and Brad (case #6) may both have known of children who had to leave class to go do testing with the psychologist. It is more likely, therefore, that your child may know of someone else who saw a psychologist and made some comments about that. Ask what they think might happen. Children many times have some images they may not feel completely comfortable sharing at first. However, after some prompting they may tell you what they think. Brad, for example, might tell you that when you are really "cool" you get to get out of class to go see the psych person. Kelly (case #3), though, might say that only the "weirdos" go see psychologists and she is afraid the other children in her class will tease her if they find out she is being tested.

Children at different ages think very differently. Preschool children as well as early elementary schoolchildren tend to see everything as it involves them and tend to see things concretely. Your discussion about what would happen during an evaluation needs to match that. Kelly (case #3) is in first grade, and Lisa (case #2) is in preschool. Any explanation to these two girls about what psychological testing would be like might include the time of the day the appointment is scheduled, where the office is, the name and gender of the psychologist, and some of the activities that might be done. For example, "Dr. Smith is a man who has an office in that building across from the grocery store. We will see him Thursday morning right after breakfast. Your teachers have already said it is OK to miss school that day; they will send home any assignments. Dr. Smith won't stick you with needles or take your temperature or anything like that. He will talk with you, maybe play some games, ask you lots of different kinds of questions, maybe do puzzles, and maybe some other things that you may never have seen before. I'll be waiting for you the whole time, though it may take all morning before you get done."

In contrast, Brian (case #8) is fifteen years old. His therapist could explain that people begin thinking of harming themselves when something inside is truly bothering them. Psychological testing can help to find out what that "thing" might be and maybe give some clues on how to help Brian feel better about it. For example, "Brian, you and I have been talking for several meetings now about how badly you feel. You even admitted that you think a lot about hurting yourself or hurting somebody. There must be something really important and really difficult to understand or handle going on with you to make you feel that way. I think that the testing can maybe give us some ideas about things that may be causing these feelings and thoughts that neither of us have considered before."

Additionally with Brian, the issue of caring can and should be communicated as it should be with all children. Statements could be made to him that go something like this: "I know that sometimes you don't care much for or about yourself and you don't believe anyone else does. But I do care about you and what happens to you, and I will work to keep you safe." This communicates caring and builds trust. Finding a way to say to children that actions are being taken out of a sense of caring can help them to accept and cooperate with evaluations and treatment.

It is important when preparing a child for testing, as when preparing for any stressful situation, not to try to minimize his or her fears. Telling a child there is nothing to be frightened of, or telling him or her simply not to worry is not only ineffective, but it also can make the child feel as if his or her feelings are not important or are wrong. Statements that begin with a parent first saying he or she understands that the child may be frightened or worried, and that is natural, show an acceptance of the feelings, as well as support for the child.

Tommy (case #1) may be very worried about what the testing will be like, especially since he is being tested because everyone seems to know he is "lousy" in math. Responding to those worries is important. His parents might say, "It can be scary going to see a new doctor for the first time, especially when you don't know what she's like or what she's going to ask you to do. I bet you think she's going to make you do all kinds of those math problems!" Waiting here for some responses and then being supportive can help allay Tommy's fears so that he can handle the situation.

When Should a Child Be Told?

A general rule of thumb is to use the child's age to determine the number of days for preparation. A five-year-old can be told five days in advance. Many children still will not remember on the day of the appointment. A short reminder on that day is helpful. There is no need to reiterate the preparation once the child has heard it. There will still be anxiety since the child does not know what the doctor looks like or what exactly will happen. But much of the fear should be dissipated.

It is also important that parents attempt to ensure that their child is well rested before any testing sessions. Many psychologists prefer doing testing in the morning as children seem more alert and rested. This is especially true if children have been in school working all morning and then need to go work and perform in a testing session all afternoon. Similarly, children should be well nourished before any testing.

Who Should Go?

The examiner may suggest who should bring the child. If not, the child should be brought by someone whom the child trusts, preferably the parent (or caregiver) who has prepared him or her for testing. There should be enough time allotted so that no one is rushed and the adult can wait if the child so desires. Often it is a good idea to bring work or reading to keep occupied while waiting the hours it may take. It is advisable that the child not arrive with siblings or friends in order to ease the process of separation when the child has to leave to go with the examiner.

What Do I Tell Siblings?

It is important to give some thought to what to tell a child's siblings about the testing. Siblings typically have a range of emotions regarding their brother's or sister's situation. They may be scared that if they don't listen to Mom or Dad, they will be brought to some doctor for testing. They may be jealous of the attention their brother or sister is getting from Mom and Dad. They may be relieved to know that finally someone is doing something about a problem they have recognized for a while.

In the same way that it is important to be honest with the child being tested, it is important to be honest in an appropriate way with siblings. In Kelly's case, it would be appropriate to explain that the family pediatrician (who all siblings tend to know) recommended the testing because Kelly gets stomachaches so often and is having problems at nighttime. The psychologist might be able to help everyone understand why she is having those problems.

Related to talking to the siblings about testing, children who are being tested might wonder what they should say to their friends or relatives. It is difficult to know how to respond when someone like Tommy (case #1) asks, "What should I tell my friends when they want to know where I was today?" In part, a parent's response needs to match the child's concerns. A child should not be forced to tell people something that is relatively private. For example, Tommy should not feel he needs to tell his friends where he was or what he was doing. However, he may have truly enjoyed himself during the testing session or thought some parts of it were pretty interesting. He may wish to tell his friends about the puzzles he did or the games he played in the office. Helping children respond in ways that are comfortable for them is probably the most helpful thing parents can do in such a situation.

It is impossible for parents to remove all stress and anxiety from their children. But, with empathic understanding, parents can help their children cope with what can be an anxious time for everyone in the family. One of the most difficult things to do as a parent at times is to accept a child's feelings without changing the situation. If José (case #4) did not want to go to be tested and was adamant about that, some parents might try their hardest to convince him that it is a good thing, it won't hurt, etc. However, those parents might say, "I know that you are frightened and this can be a frightening thing, but — ." Making statements such as this acknowledges that his feelings are real. That acknowledgment alone can many times be a tremendous help in preparing children not only for psychological evaluations, but any life stress.

6

Waiting and Wondering, "What's Happening to My Child?"

How do other kids do on this?
— Seven-year-old girl being tested in school

What's the right answer to this one anyway?
— Ten-year-old boy in a school psychologist's office

WATCHING a child go through an examination of some sort is a difficult thing for many parents. Parents have different reactions; some parents actually find that they need to turn away or not watch their child. Others want to jump in and help or encourage their child. This is especially so when others are present or when the results have important implications for the child or family. It may be easier for parents to let their child go into a psychologist's office and not watch what happens. However, then imagination can take over as parents fantasize about what is taking place, what the results will show, and whether good

81

or bad will occur. Parents may wonder if the psychologist will blame them for the problems, or may already feel as if they are to blame. Thus, parents sit and wonder what is being "done to" their child?

Sometimes parents may have a sense that there is an "invasion of privacy" going on; that personal or family "secrets" will not be secret. No parent truly wants to hear of a child's negative feelings toward them, even though they are normal (this is evidenced by the five-year-old boy who commented to his mother in a restaurant, "Gee, this is romantic, I love you *and* hate you!"). We wonder if our child will make statements that can be misunderstood, or whether the child will leave the evaluation feeling upset or hurt.

Psychological testing as part of an assessment process is not magic. The image often seen on prime-time television of the psychologist sitting back and asking strange and ir- relevant questions regardless of the reason for the child's being in the office is misleading. Psychological testing is not painful, and children tend to leave feeling as if they have had a reasonably good experience. Psychologists are alert to "failure experiences" as a possibility during an evaluation and address them in a manner that attempts to leave children feeling good about the testing experi- ence as a whole. The more information an evaluator has, the better he or she can organize the tests and tasks so the child avoids leaving on a note of failure. Also, psy- chologists for the most part are not allowed (because of test standardization) to tell children if they were right or wrong. So sometimes children are not even aware of how well they have done. The testing situation is an evaluative one, not a judgmental one.

The kinds of activities done in a psychological testing session are well thought out. Children are not asked to do activities that are aimlessly or arbitrarily put together. Rather, the tasks/tests administered, the questions asked, the games played, and the behavior observed all serve the purpose of gaining insight into the child so as to answer questions.

What Types of Tests May Be Used?

Intelligence Tests

The most frequently and widely used tests are intelligence tests. The origins of intelligence testing go back to the nineteenth century where scientists interested in intellectual differences between people were attempting to develop various tests. Alfred Binet, working in France, was charged with designing a method whereby slower (retarded) students could be identified and educated differently. His work led to the early forms of intelligence testing. Binet believed that testing was one part or one aspect of helping understand children's abilities.

Since 1905, intelligence tests have been used to decide such issues as school placement, understanding thinking, finding talents, and selection. The principle behind the test is to evaluate where the person fits as compared to others of his or her age in areas of thinking, reasoning, judgment, memory, visual motor activity, and vocabulary. The IQ is a summary number that describes the position a person is in relative to his or her peers.

Intelligence tests have been and continue to be widely used in schools to help in determining the presence of a learning disability, mental retardation, developmental delays, giftedness, or other questions related to school performance. These tests have come under criticism for racial/cultural bias. For example, in California an IQ test cannot be used as the basis for placement in a special education classroom because a state court decided that there was bias against minority students, which resulted in significantly more minority students in special classes.

Bias can occur in at least two ways. The norms of the test can be developed in such a manner that some particular groups of children score either higher or lower than the standardization group. Bias can also occur in the use of the test results. Test results must therefore be interpreted in a context. If we know that a particular group tends to score lower on a test and that the test is probably "biased" against that group, the significance of the scores should be interpreted differently. If they are taken at face value, then there is bias in the interpretation as well. In spite of the political issues surrounding the appropriate use of IQ tests, in the hands of a well-trained psychologist who evaluates the results in terms of cultural background, they can yield a great deal of useful information.

A caution should be included here regarding the actual IQ score. Many parents as well as other professionals place a great deal of emphasis on what the "IQ" is. However, as mentioned earlier in this chapter, the IQ is a summary score that gives an average across a variety of skills. As such, it can be very misleading if used as a major descriptor of a child. All people have strengths and weaknesses; some tasks are easy while others prove difficult or beyond our grasp. The profile of strengths and weaknesses that is unique for every child is more useful than the summary IQ. The profile can lead to recommendations for interventions in terms of teaching, managing behavior, and solving problems. Well-trained psychologists examine the profile of strengths and weaknesses as a way to understand a child more thoroughly. They always will describe in their reports what that profile is like.

Two of the most widely used individually administered intelligence tests are the Wechsler Scales (Wechsler Preschool and Primary Scale of Intelligence-Revised, Wechsler Intelligence Scale for Children-III, and Wechsler Adult Intelligence Scale-Revised) and the Stanford-Binet Intelligence Scale, Fourth Edition. These are all individually administered and require training to administer and to interpret. There are also many other IQ and cognitive processing tests that might be chosen in addition to or in place of these major ones. Parents interested in listings of various intelligence tests (as well as other psychological tests) can find an extensive listing in Anastasi (1988). A table listing tests commonly used with children and adolescents is included in the appendix of this book as well.

Group intelligence tests are occasionally administered in schools by teachers or other school personnel. These tests (such as the Otis-Lennon, or the Cognitive Abilities Test) do not bill themselves as "intelligence" test. Rather, they call themselves aptitude or general ability tests. Still, they do resemble intelligence tests in their attempt to assess cognitive abilities in children through paper-and-pencil techniques. These measures are not used too often by psychologists conducting psychological testing of children.

Achievement Testing

Achievement tests are measures designed to evaluate how much a child has learned or how much he or she knows about a particular subject area. These tests typically parallel the subjects taught in school (e.g., reading, math, social studies, etc.) and are organized by grade level and age. Items on the test or subtest begin with questions normally taught in the early grades and then proceed on with questions about ideas, facts, etc., taught in the later grades. The resulting scores are presented in percentiles, grade equivalents, or stanines (see chapter 7 for a further description of test scores).

Achievement tests only assess what children have been able to learn up to the time of testing. They do not measure whether a child *can* learn, nor what sort of potential a child may have to learn various kinds of material. Furthermore, they do not assess performance in school. A child who scores above grade level on an achievement test may not be performing in class as if he or she were above grade level. In fact, a child can be receiving failing grades and still have achievement scores that demonstrate adequate learning. Achievement test scores must be examined in conjunction with other information that is available about a child.

Achievement testing is primarily conducted in school systems, with the tests administered by the teachers and/or their aids. They are usually given in a large group format in the classroom. The score sheets are then sent off for scoring and the results sent back by the various testing corporations. As parents of elementary schoolchildren, you are probably familiar with these procedures and with the various tests the school systems use. These tests give a general picture of achievement and help identify those who may be having difficulty learning.

When questions of learning or school performance are present, psychologists will administer *individual* achievement tests to children. The format differs somewhat in that the tests are developed and geared to be used in a one-to-one situation in an office where the psychologist can closely observe performance. The directions are highly standardized, but still allow for rapport to be established, and for the evaluator to make judgments about the accuracy of the data. Psychologists also integrate the information from an achievement test with other information they have collected so that a clear and detailed portrait of the child emerges from the testing.

There are advantages as well as disadvantages to individually administered testing. The major advantages relate to learning about the child and how he or she went about solving the problem or completing the various items. The psychologist can observe the process the child was using. It is also possible to go back and review with the child certain areas of difficulty to learn whether the child could be shown how to complete the items, whether they could be completed if presented differently, etc. This is typically referred to as "testing the limits," and is only done after the formal testing is completed. One obvious disadvantage is that individually administered tests are more time consuming. They take longer and are impractical for use in school systems where all children must be tested for academic and curriculum purposes. Also, many individually administered achievement tests are specialized measures of skill areas that offer in-depth analysis of strengths and weaknesses. The Keymath-Revised and the Test of Written Language-Revised are frequently used examples of such measures.

Individually administered achievement tests have other advantages over group tests. Some individual tests (e.g., Peabody Individual Achievement Test-Revised) attempt to eliminate or reduce verbal responses. With these measures, items are visual in nature and ask the child to answer by selecting from a set of pictures following the item. These measures are useful when the psychologist suspects that the child may be having difficulties in other areas (e.g., hearing, language) that might interfere with the measurement of achievement. In performing classroom tasks, the psychologist can then observe in detail how the child processes information and expresses himself or herself.

Perceptual Motor Measures

There is also a group of measures used in psychological evaluations that assesses how well children are able to coordinate what they see with what they can draw or copy. These are the perceptual-motor measures. Perceptual-motor measures look at a child's ability to perceive correctly (see and understand) symbols and shapes, and to reproduce those symbols and shapes. As children grow, their ability to draw what they see and to copy increasingly complex symbols improves markedly. This development provides the child with some of the skills involved in learning how to read, to print, and eventually to write. There are also measures that do not require the child to copy any forms physically. Rather, the child is asked to match designs or select the correct match from an array.

These kinds of tools help to assess perceptual skills apart from any motor (drawing) skills.

Perceptual-motor measures, such as the Bender Visual Motor Gestalt Test, or the Beery-Buktenica Developmental Test of Visual Motor Integration, are usually administered individually to evaluate these processes. These measures "screen" for neurological problems. Children who have significant trouble reproducing the designs in these tests (that others their age produce with ease) may have cognitive or perceptual processing problems. It must be stressed, though, that when someone uses these measures as a screening tool they are by *no means* definitive. While perceptual-motor tests give us important information about a child, they cannot by themselves diagnose any disorders. As with all tests included in psychological batteries, the results must be integrated with other data and interpreted by a skilled and well-trained psychologist.

Personality, Social, and Behavioral Measures

Webster's New World Dictionary defines personality as:

> habitual patterns and qualities of behavior of any individual as expressed by physical and mental activities and attitudes; distinctive individual qualities of a person considered collectively.

Personality testing varies depending upon the definition of personality held by the psychologist. As a result, there are a wide variety of measures that have been developed to assess personality. In general, personality testing is an attempt to understand how people typically cope with the world, including how they see themselves, how they see and relate to others, how they deal with stress and conflicts, and what their emotional lives are like. Some of the strategies for measuring personality will be explored here.

One way that psychologists have looked at personality is through what are called "projective" tests. In these kinds of tests, the person is shown some vague material and asked to respond to it. For example he or she may be shown a picture of a boy sitting alone and be asked to tell a story about the picture. The theory behind these tests is that whatever is in the story is related to the person's unique interests, concerns, and personality. The psychologist's job is then to interpret the story as it might relate to the client's life. Other examples are the inkblot test (the Rorschach) where a person is asked to tell what an inkblot could look like and the incomplete sentences test where a person is asked to complete sentences, such as, "When I am unhappy, I...."

Another way that personality is measured is through "objective" tests. Here, the person may be given a questionnaire and asked to respond to each item in terms of how much it describes or applies to them. The results are then tallied and scores for various personality dimensions are assigned and compared to norms. Objective measures are very different in approach from the projective tests. Both, though, are attempting to describe the important features of a person's personality.

Measuring personality in children has always been difficult. In the personality assessment of young children, objective personality measures are often inappropriate because of the reading ability taking these tests requires. As a result, psychologists tend to rely more on projective measures and interview data to get an assessment of personality. It is common to ask children to draw different things as a way to get a reading on their perception of their life. Drawings of houses, trees, and people are commonly requested of children, as are drawings of families, schools, and free-form drawings of anything the child wants.

Understanding children through their drawings does not depend, as many people believe, on the artistic ability of the child (or the adult, for that matter). There is normative information on the development of drawings that is used in interpreting the drawings based on clinical experience. Clearly, however, use of these kinds of measures is limited, and no major decisions can be confidently made based solely on one or two of these tests.

When a child is old enough to read without difficulty, he or she can be given self-report measures. For example, Brian (case #8) is an adolescent. For him, paper-and-pencil personality questionnaires might be appropriate. He could be given the Minnesota Multiphasic Personality Inventory-2 (MMPI-2), an objective measure of personality, or the Beck Depression Inventory (BDI), a symptom checklist.

Because it is difficult to get reliable self reports from young children about their personality, there is a greater use of observational data, often collected through structured test formats completed by both parents and teachers. One such test is the Child Behavior Checklist. In measures such as this, a questionnaire is filled out by parents or teachers (and in some cases, by the child himself or herself on a self-report form). The items describe a variety of problem behaviors and the teacher or parent is asked to rate the frequency with which the child engages in that behavior. There are different forms for different age groups, different scoring norms for boys and girls, and different versions for use in school or home. An advantage to these measures is that they allow the comparison between how a child acts in school versus home.

Another behavior checklist that provides useful information is the Connors' Rating Scale. This too is a measure filled out by teachers and parents. It assesses a variety of personality and behavioral features, including attention problems. It is frequently used in evaluations where there is a question of attention deficit disorder (hyperactivity). It has both parent and teacher forms with extended and abbreviated versions.

Behavior checklists and questionnaires are becoming more and more frequently used by psychologists. Parents who have a child being evaluated either by a school psychologist or a psychologist in independent practice may well be asked to fill out several lengthy forms. Teachers or others who know a child well may also be asked to fill out one or several of these rating forms. Again, the advantage is that it is possible to get a description of a child across a range of settings.

Besides the formal testing and checklists psychologists might use to gain insight into a child, they also talk with children. Simply sitting and talking with, and listening to a child, can help reveal concerns and issues that the child believes to be important. Many times what a child thinks important is not what the parents or others who made the referral believe is important. For example, teachers might be very concerned about José's (case #4) lack of attention in the classroom. Yet, when talking with José, he may be more concerned about making friends in a new country and when his aunt and uncle will allow him to try to contact his parents in his home country.

While not considered part of psychological *testing,* there is an interview procedure used by psychologists and psychiatrists when a psychiatric diagnosis is needed. This interview is known as a Mental Status Examination. Unlike psychological testing and its emphasis on standardization, normative data, and psychometrics, the mental status exam is a semistructured interview. It is used to assess, among other things, a person's mood, affect or emotions, thought processes, ability to relate, memory for recent and distant events, and abstract reasoning. Psychological test data, particularly from personality testing, can be very helpful when combined with mental status examination results. Together, the information from these techniques can help provide a psychiatric diagnosis, if that has been requested, as well as help develop an understanding of the child.

In addition to projective measures of personality, social, and behavioral checklists or procedures, interviews, and self-ratings, psychologists observe children. These observations usually begin from the moment of introduction and continue throughout the evaluation. In addition to the observations done during the testing procedures, some observations may be done in the classroom as well. If the referral is school based, as with José, a psychologist might spend some time in the school observing the child in class as well as at play/recess. During these times it is important to remember that the evaluator would not only be watching the child being assessed; the classroom as it forms the context for the behavior will also be observed. This helps to gain an understanding of the demands placed upon children and gives information of value in interpreting the tests.

Observing the child in a classroom often takes on added importance when placement is involved in the referral question. Tommy (case #1) presents an excellent example where observing him in his classes, both in math and in other classes, would provide very important information. If the recommendation would be for a different kind of classroom, or a different school altogether, having information based on classroom observation in the psychological report may be crucial. Describing how a child functions in a group or in groups of various sizes adds to a report and to the weight of the recommendations. As mentioned earlier, the context of development is crucial to understand if we are to understand children. Spending time observing children in their various contexts, when the referral warrants, adds greatly to the report and the recommendations. These observations are often done before more formal testing has started since children can be on their best behavior when they know someone will be watching how they are doing.

A common way for school psychologists to begin an assessment of a child is to review the records and then observe the child in class. Again, this would be done before formal testing would be scheduled. In the private sector, parents may need to discuss whether observations of a child are necessary, since it can add on substantial expense to the cost of an independent evaluation. Sometimes it is possible for information from an observation done by a psychologist in the school system to be shared with someone from outside the system who is doing testing. However, if it is decided that actually seeing the child in his or her environment is needed, efforts should be made to see that it can be accomplished.

Adaptive Behavior

It is often important to have a way of determining how well a person is adjusting or adapting to his or her living situations. The questions here range from whether a person can take care of his or her own personal hygiene to whether he or she can manage a household and job responsibly. This area is critical to assessments involving questions of mental retardation since mental retardation is currently defined as below-average intelligence coupled with below average adaptive skills.

Measuring adaptive behavior is done most commonly through interview procedures where the evaluator uses a set of descriptions of skills and behaviors and determines whether the individual can do those skills. For example, the Vineland Adaptive Behavior Scales is a lengthy listing of items grouped according to communication, daily living, and socialization skills. The list of behaviors begins with those that very young children should be able to do, such as smiling at a caregiver or remembering an important person's name, and progress on to sophisticated behaviors, such as not making fun of people in public, not monopolizing conversations, and budgeting money. The evaluator interviews someone who knows the person being evaluated very well and gathers information about these skills. A similar measure is the American Association of Mental Deficiency Adaptive Scale. Here too, a person is assessed to determine the level of sophistication of his or her self-care and management skills.

An advantage of these kinds of measures is that

they are relatively objective, describe behaviors and skills clearly, can be filled out through interviews with knowledgeable people, and provide developmental levels concerning a person's adaptation. It also helps the evaluator to describe more precisely what an individual's strengths and weaknesses may be. These measures are commonly used when there is a question about mental retardation or level of retardation, or when an estimate of a person's functional levels is important to know.

Neuropsychological Tests and Measures of Cognitive Functions

Neuropsychological evaluation includes the administration of a comprehensive battery (or group) of tests that were compiled in order to provide a thorough assessment of brain functions. Typically, these batteries are lengthy, requiring three to four hours (or more) to complete. The goal is to measure a wide range of human skills and behaviors in order to assess how well different parts of a person's brain are functioning. Neuropsychological testing is recommended when there may be reason to suspect that some neurological deficit is present (for example, because a child suffered a head injury or serious disease), or when a highly fine-grained analysis of cognitive, perceptual, or motor functions is required.

A neuropsychological battery (such as the Halstead-Reitan or the Luria-Nebraska) usually includes an IQ test, such as one of those discussed earlier in this chapter, and will often include an achievement test, perceptual measures, and behavioral observations or checklists. They will often include other measures of cognitive abilities. Tests such as the Woodcock-Johnson-Revised Tests of Cognitive Abilities are common additions in neuropsychological testing. These measures help to break down cognitive processing into more basic components and allow the neuropsychologist to develop a better idea regarding the type of difficulty a child might be having.

In addition, supplemental measures of skills, such as, memory, concept formation, fine motor skills, gross motor skills, hand dominance, foot dominance, visual field, language processing, auditory processing, etc., will frequently be used. The benefit of these lengthy (and sometimes expensive) batteries is that they are highly comprehensive. Still, there are times that even with that extensive testing, there are no easy or clear-cut answers to the referral questions.

Vocational, Interests, Career Measures

Interests and career measures look at how closely a particular individual's interests match those of people who have been in various careers. The goal is to gather information that can help a person make decisions about further education, choice of college major, or vocational training. Some vocational testing, typically done by experts in vocational assessment, take the person through a series of tasks that resemble or sample real work experiences. For example, some motor tasks may be given to assess mechanical aptitude. The result is a description of work skills that a person has.

Interest inventories, unlike vocational assessment, evaluate how a person's interests parallel those of people with particular occupations. The Strong-Campbell Interest Inventory, for example, will tell people how closely their interests match the interests of people in careers ranging from architects to zoo keepers. That information, in conjunction with career counseling can be used to provide guidance in choosing a college or a major in college, as well as a high-school program that will give the foundations needed for these fields. Julie (case #9) is someone who could benefit greatly from these kinds of measures.

When the referral question is centered around post-secondary educational placement, particularly with high-school students, vocational or interest measures may be used. It is common for vocational rehabilitation systems to request not only aptitude testing, but also vocational or interests assessment before they agree to fund a student for either college or vocational training. These measures, in conjunction with counseling, can help a student make a decision about college and career choices, as well as vocational training. They can be useful with high-school students as well as students at the postsecondary level.

How Will the Tests Be Selected?

Psychologists will select the tests to be included in a battery (group of tests) primarily to address the referral question or questions and the decisions that parents need to make. There are some measures, though, that are almost universally given regardless of the question. An IQ test is typically administered because the information about a child's cognitive strengths and weaknesses is useful in most cases. Having an understanding of a child's cognitive skills (i.e., intelligence) can provide a useful framework for understanding other psychological processes. Interviews with the parents or teachers, and with the child are also practically universal, despite the referral question or problem.

A psychologist will select tests that allow him or her to compare the child in question with other children of the same age or age range. For example, there are three versions of the Wechsler scales, one for preschool children, one for elementary- and high-school-aged children, and one for adults. Most tests of cognitive processing, as well as measures of social behaviors (i.e., the behavior checklists) have some age range on which they focus. The age range needs to be appropriate for the child in question.

Other considerations in selecting a test will depend upon the unique characteristics of the child. Children who are from minority groups, particularly when the minority is a non-English-speaking group, will need special tests. When working with minority groups, the psychologist will need to ensure that the tests selected have normative or standardization groups that include the minority of the child being tested. It is not appropriate to compare a child from one particular subgroup of society only with children from other (majority) groups.

When children have special needs, such as sensory impairments (visual or hearing), physical limitations, language problems, etc., the tests are selected so that the data is not confounded by those other impairments. For example, some items from the Wechsler scales are timed, with bonus points awarded for speedy completion. A youngster with cerebral palsy, such as Julie (case #9), which can affect fine motor skills, would not be able to earn those bonus points, even though he or she may have quickly understood how to solve or complete the test item.

Therefore, the results would underestimate Julie's true cognitive abilities because of her physical limitations.

Once the special and unique considerations of each child have been considered, the psychologist returns to the referral question(s). He or she would then need to choose whether a formal assessment procedure is necessary or whether an informal procedure would provide the needed information. There are times when a complete testing battery is not necessary and enough information to be helpful can be gathered from interviewing the parents and the child. Other times, the question to be answered requires more formal test procedures.

A goal of much personality assessment is to arrive at a diagnosis. While there is disagreement in the field regarding the usefulness of diagnosing children and the system to use when diagnosing, it is still a common request. In fact, many insurance companies, if they pay for psychological testing, expect and require a diagnosis before processing a reimbursement. Personality testing can be an aid in determining not only cognitive "diagnoses" (such as Developmental Reading Disorder), but in psychiatric diagnoses as well. Personality and behavioral assessment can help make diagnoses such as anxiety disorders, pervasive developmental disorders, conduct disorders, and other psychiatric disturbances. These diagnoses will typically be included in a report in a "diagnostic" section.

What about Reliability and Validity?

Psychological testing and assessment often play major roles in life decisions. Therefore, having test results that we can trust and that we believe are accurate is of the utmost importance. It is highly unlikely that we would get exactly the same scores on a child when the tests are repeated two or three times. Yet, we do not expect the scores to change significantly unless a major life event occurred between testings.

Two of the most important issues in testing and assessment are reliability and validity. They are often confused. Reliability refers to how much we trust the results of the measurement; if we tested the person again, would we obtain about the same results? No measure in psychology, nor in other fields, has perfect reliability. People watching their weight often know that if they get off a scale and stand back on it a second time the reading may change somewhat. In psychology too, an IQ obtained on a Monday morning may not be the same as that obtained on a Thursday afternoon.

Because of the importance of a test's reliability and the difficulty in measuring it, test developers go to great lengths to increase or improve the reliability of a test before it is published. One way they do this is to be sure that the administration procedures are exasperatingly clear. This reduces the error that might be introduced because different people administer the test differently. The same is true for the scoring, which should be very clear. It is also true that a long test tends to be more reliable than a short test. Reliability also needs to be established at each age level, since children of different ages perform in different ways on similar tasks.

Professional guidelines for test users and developers published by several professional associations require psychologists to use only those instruments where adequate reliability has been established. Thus, it is the responsibility of the psychologist to consider test reliability in selection. However, other factors are of equal importance.

Another characteristic of a test that a psychologist is aware of is validity. Validity, unlike reliability, does not rest in the test itself. Rather, validity relates to the *use* to which a test is put. For example, one inappropriate use of psychological testing would be in using the inkblot test, a personality measure, to determine aptitude for college achievement. The inkblot test has no validity in use with measuring college achievement. A medical analogy might be asking for a CBC (comprehensive blood count) as a way to determine if a person has a broken arm. The CBC is not valid for use in determining bone structure. However, it is completely valid for determining blood composition.

A validity argument that psychologists take up frequently is whether a test truly is measuring what it claims to be measuring. Does an intelligence test really measure intelligence, or does it measure some other trait? Does a test really measure depression, or does it measure a tendency to respond to questions about depression? These issues or questions must be answered in a satisfactory manner before a test is used in any assessment battery. If a psychologist is to make statements based on test data about a child's cognitive strengths and weaknesses, he or she must be confident that the measures used truly reflect those skills that the test purports to measure in the test manual.

Examples

As mentioned before, measures would be chosen to fit particular needs. Therefore, it is hard to present a battery of tests that would be used in all situations. However, a few possible batteries are suggested here for some of the children described in chapter 1.

The evaluation of Tommy (case #1) involves ruling out or describing a learning disability in math. A possible battery could include the Wechsler Intelligence Scale for Children-III, the math subtests from the Woodcock Johnson Tests of Achievement-Revised, and the Developmental Test of Visual Motor Integration as a start. These measures would look at general cognitive strengths and weaknesses as well as visual-motor integration. Based on these preliminary results, further cognitive assessment could be carried out with the Woodcock-Johnson-Revised Tests of Cognitive Abilities to get a further and more fine-grained analysis of how Tommy thinks and approaches problem solving. If there seemed to be an emotional component, such as Tommy reacts very strongly to his math teacher or is reacting to events at home, projective drawings as well as a behavior checklist might be helpful.

In contrast, Brad (case #6) has a more complicated presenting problem. There are reports of attention problems, hostility, variable academic performance, and poor peer relationships. This could be a severe learning disability; it could also be an emotional disturbance. Therefore, a very complete battery would be needed, including intelligence testing, visual-motor integration, in-depth assessments of memory, language, and other cognitive functions, and interviews with teachers (perhaps also asking teachers and the child's mother to fill out one or more of the various checklists for problem behaviors). However, this would not be enough. Personality testing would be critical with Brad. The use of projective drawings, along with other more sophisticated projective techniques and perhaps a play interview, coupled with observations, might all be necessary to assess Brad's difficulties accurately.

For José (case #4), measures that require attention would be important to give, since the major complaint is that he is distractible. Some of the cognitive and memory tests require attention and would be appropriate. Questionnaires and behavior checklists that contain questions focusing on a child's ability to attend in various situations (such as the Connors' Rating Scale) would also be critical here. Since the background information about José's uncle has been withheld, there is little reason to think automatically of something psychiatrically contributing to his difficulties, although it would still need to be ruled out with personality testing. Interviews with his caregivers would be important in focusing on situations that can induce stress and, thus, impair attention and concentration.

Julie (case #9) presents a different kind of dilemma. Her cerebral palsy impairs her physically, and therefore, measures that do not require speedy performance would be most appropriate. There are measures of intelligence that could be used with Julie (parts of the Stanford-Binet Intelligence Scale, the verbal portion of the Wechsler Adult Intelligence Scale-Revised, or selected cognitive subtests from the Woodcock-Johnson-Revised Tests of Cognitive Abilities would be useful) to assess her reasoning skills separate from her fine motor performance. There are also perceptual measures that do not require a physical or motor response that would be helpful. And, because she is at a college age and thinking of careers, one of the interest inventories could be beneficial. The evaluator may have to assist Julie in making the kinds of responses necessary (e.g., filling in the answer sheet for her).

In general, infants present still different problems. Assessing infants is a tricky business and the measures often lack reliability or predictability. However, it is possible through different behavior scales to assess development. The strategy is to determine first what kinds of skills babies have (and they have many!) at different ages, and then find a way to elicit them. Searching for a familiar voice, for example, develops quite early and can be assessed. Furthermore, we know that reflexes present at birth (such as turning the head to the side when the cheek is stroked) drop out or fade as a child grows. When they do not fade and can be elicited when the child is older, we assume his or her development is not proceeding normally.

How Is My Child Doing?

As you as a parent sit and wonder what your child is doing and how well he or she is doing it, try to keep in mind that tests are simply tasks that your child works on. Some tasks will be fun, others boring; some will be easy, others very challenging. But, beyond those tasks, a skilled examiner is doing more than simply administering these tasks. He or she is watching the child's reaction to the situation, the ability to persevere with difficult tasks, the strategies used in approaching the problem. Further, the examiner is watching how the child relates to the examiner himself or herself. Does the child chat and relate comfortably? Does the child seem shy, timid, and withdrawn? Is he or she enthused about the activities or overwhelmed and resistant?

The process of doing an assessment is a complicated one. Training and supervision are required to be able to do the job thoroughly and well. The product of all this work, then, should be an understanding of the particular child in question. That understanding, in the best of all worlds, is complete and comprehensive. In reality, though, it often continues to have gaps that cannot be filled by a onetime evaluation.

It cannot be emphasized strongly enough that psychological testing is only a *sample* of behavior. To the extent that the sample represents a child's typical daily functioning, the testing will be an accurate reflection of the child. However, when for whatever reason, the sample does not represent the daily functioning of a child (e.g., the child is sick, is missing his favorite television program, is worried about being hurt by the doctor) the testing will not be accurate. This is why test data must be integrated with other knowledge about the child to determine its accuracy and usefulness.

7

What about the Results?

When do I find out how I did?
— Thirteen-year-old applying
for a gifted and talented program

PSYCHOLOGICAL assessment is not completed until the test results have been shared. As the assessment was undertaken to answer specific concerns, it is customary to return to the referral question(s) in a report. Although results may be communicated orally, particularly when necessary to expedite implementation of some form of intervention or service, a written report should always follow. A written psychological report may continue to influence the life of the individual assessed for years, particularly if it becomes part of school or personnel records. As such, it should be well written and reviewed with care and with consideration for all available information and intervening circumstances, as well as with respect for the individual.

This chapter focuses on answers to typical questions regarding the reporting of test results.

From Whom Do I Get Results?

Results are usually reported by the individual who did the testing. However, a parent or the individual who has been tested may receive the results "second hand." For example, in Brian's case (#8), the court received a psychological evaluation for its own use in decision making. Thus, results will be given directly to the judge. Direct interpretation of results to Brian or his family may be by a court-appointed social worker or youth counselor, rather than by the psychologist who completed the evaluation. Similarly, results from evaluations requested by various agencies may not always be shared directly with the individual or immediate family. In case #8, Brian's psychotherapist has suggested psychological testing to assist in treatment planning. The request will be made by the judge to Protective Services, as Brian is a foster child under their care. Results will be shared with them, as well as with the psychotherapist and court, in this situation. Brian most likely will receive interpretation of test results as part of the ongoing process of therapy.

When testing has been completed by a school, the method of reporting the results varies. Public schools do not pursue psychological testing without obtaining permission; thus, results of school psychological testing are always reported (usually verbally as well as in written form) directly to parents/guardians. The written psychological report will remain a part of the child's confidential school record (see chapters 8 and 9). Results may initially be shared in a parent meeting, with other school personnel present. Although a rare occurrence, it is possible that someone other than the school psychologist who completed the testing may present the results. However, parents may request copies of school test results prior to meeting with school staff. When the school recommends testing and refers a student elsewhere, the parent will almost always be responsible for scheduling and financial arrangements. In these situations, the parent receives the results from the private psychological examiner first and decides whether to share them with the school (see chapters 8 and 9).

When testing is part of a private school admissions process, a brief, written report is usually supplied. However, when questions arise, parents may request a meeting with the examiner to discuss results further.

When individuals or parents seek testing on their own, as Julie in case #9 or Jeremy's parents in case #5, reports are always shared directly with the parents. As an eighteen-year-old, Julie may make her own arrangements for testing and control the use of test results. Jeremy's parents, also, would be the first to know the opinions and recommendations of the psychological examiner.

How can I Comprehend an Oral Report of Test Results?

Comprehension of orally presented information depends upon the level of familiarity with the concepts and terms used. Thus, anyone who does not have training as a psychologist is at a disadvantage in an "informing" conference (where testing results are described). Keep in mind that the stated purpose of such a conference is to share test results. Participants should be ready to take an active role as consumers of psychological services. Prior to the conference, it may be helpful to prepare specific questions for which answers are expected. Some examples include:

- How did my child react to being tested?
- Were there any factors that negatively affected testing?
- What can you tell me about each test?
- What strengths did testing reveal?
- What problem areas were revealed by testing?
- What do test results imply about functioning at home, school, work, and in social situations?
- Exactly what should be done now?

General suggestions for "surviving" an oral report of test results include:

- Asking for definitions of unfamiliar terms (see the glossary of this book for help).
- Requesting examples to support generalizations posited by the psychologist.
- Offering examples that you think contradict test results in order to allow an opportunity for explanation.
- Asking for repetition of information you did not "catch" when first presented.
- Requesting a summary before leaving.

What Should I Expect in a Written Report?

While there will be variability in the format and style of the written reports of psychological test results due to differences in the training, purpose, personal preferences, and theoretical orientation of the psychologist, there are certain features that appear in many reports:

- Relevant identifying information (e.g., name, date[s] of testing, birth date, age, grade, examiner's name and qualifications, tests administered and other assessment procedures — such as, interviews or observations).

- Referral information including referral source, reason for referral, and questions to be answered.

- Relevant background information (developmental, medical, family, social, school and/or work history, as well as current status across areas, reports of observations, and prior test results).

- Behavioral observations or a description of what happened during testing.

- Assessment results.

- Clinical and diagnostic impressions.

- Recommendations.

- Signature.

The written report should be reviewed for inaccuracies in the identifying and background information, which may be corrected. Questions regarding assessment results, impressions, or recommendations should be addressed directly to the psychological examiner.

Parents should review a report in light of the referral question(s) that are usually stated at the beginning. This is the stated "goal" of the evaluation. The reader should find the report written in a manner that is consistent with the stated purpose of the evaluation. In particular, impressions and recommendations should specifically address the questions posed. For example, if an intelligence test is administered as part of a screening process for admission to a school program, a parent should expect a description of behavior during testing and interpretation of scores relative to observed behaviors and what is expected or "normative" for children of similar ages. Any limitations (such as fatigue, a cold, a broken arm) should be addressed. However, if no background data was available for consideration and only one test was used, the examiner may lack the context and comparisons necessary to make statements about the child in terms of what might be expected.

Occasionally, parents may wish to use results from psychological testing for some purpose other than the original "goal" stated in the report. In such cases, they should consult the psychologist who completed the evaluation to discuss the use of the test results with regard to the "new goal."

Generally, there should be a new understanding of the presenting problem(s), particularly when a battery of psychological tests is used. The report should go beyond description. There should be some effort toward possible explanations for the problem behavior(s). Any areas where assessment was incomplete or where results were equivocal should be specified. After reviewing a report, the reader should be able to formulate a reasonable picture of the "whole child."

A caution needs to be interjected here. Psychological tests may lead to speculation about causes of behavior or problems in terms of underlying psychological processes. However, psychological tests cannot (and should not be expected to) discover past life events. They cannot determine if someone has been physically or sexually abused, or suffered some other sort of trauma. Using them in a detective fashion is not appropriate or helpful. The most that could be said about a child is that his or her profile of scores is similar to those of children known to have been abused. Still, this neither confirms nor refutes events in the child's life. This differs from speculating with varying degrees of confidence as to whether a learning disability or a particular psychiatric disturbance might be underlying behaviors that are observed.

What about the "Numbers"?

Numbers cannot convey dynamic impressions. They are static representations — symbols — applied to help explain the world. As symbols, they must be interpreted. Thus, efforts to explain a child's test performance through "numbers" or scores must be accompanied by interpretation in order to give them meaning. Just as isolating one still frame from a videotape of a child's life yields nothing more than a static snapshot, relying on numbers, such as IQ scores, to characterize a child's test performance gives nothing more than a static representation of that sample of the child's behavior. In both cases, explanations and interpretations are essential to give meaning to the data provided.

Numbers are not always derived in psychological assessment. The purpose of a psychological evaluation will dictate the assessment procedures chosen and the manner in which results are reported. In many situations, the assessment procedures utilized will not yield "numbers" or scores to be reported to parents. For example, Edward (case #10) and his parents may have thorough clinical interviews with the psychologist designed to determine if they are experiencing a normal grief reaction to the loss of the family dog or if Edward is manifesting behavior that reflects more enduring psychological problems. No further formal psychological testing may be suggested if it is determined that Edward and his family are experiencing grief. Thus, the psychologist's clinical impression and recommendations may be based on an interpretation of background information and clinical interview data such as the assessment procedures, not formal test data. Therefore, no "numbers" will be presented to Edward's family.

When formal psychological tests are administered as part of the assessment process, the reporting of results should focus on the meaning or interpretation of the child's performance in context. Numbers will not, in and of themselves, form the basis of a description of the "whole child." The inclusion of numbers in reports will be based on the psychologist's judgment with regard to their validity or representativeness, the role they play in addressing the referral questions, and/or their usefulness in interpretation. For example, the psychologist who tested Lisa (case #2) may not have reported scores from the Wechsler Preschool and Primary Scale of Intelligence-Revised (WPPSI-R) to her parents, as, developmentally, she was not ready for most of the tasks presented. Therefore, the scores are not felt to be "valid." Also, the psychologist reminds Lisa's parents that tests are much less reliable with young children, so her performance on this particular evaluation may not be indicative of what she will do in subsequent testing with the WPPSI-R.

If a referral question deals with admission to a special program or a situation where a preset "cutoff score" is used, the score(s) may be reported. For example, had Jeremy's (case #5) scores fallen below the high cutoff score set by private schools or gifted and talented programs for admission, he would have been found "not ready for kindergarten" by that particular school. This decision would have been based on the cutoff score chosen even though he may have scored above average on the test.

Some psychologists report scores when attempting to emphasize relative strengths or weaknesses across test results. Other psychologists will never include "numbers" in interpreting test results. Rather they will rely on explanation, describing a child's strengths and weaknesses, typical ways of coping with situations, and approach to the world.

The use of numbers may lead to problems when reported excessively or as "definitive." Too many numbers, where there is inadequate explanation and interpretation, tend to be overwhelming. The reporting of numbers as "definitive" is unfounded. There are always limitations in the testing situation and the tests, as well, which prohibit reliance on single numbers for decision making.

The most common error made in the use of tests is the application of cutoff scores for decision making, particularly where other factors are not considered. This practice fails to take into account the problems inherent in tests and measurement and is, therefore, unwarranted. In fact, caution should always be exercised in using test scores for decision making. It is the manner in which the scores were obtained, within the context of the life demands the child is facing, which makes the scores meaningful.

Even though psychologists agree that the test scores should remain secondary to interpretation, there are times that scores must be an integral part of a report of psychological testing. In fact, almost all parents are baffled at some point by the numbers included in reports of educational testing received from their child's school. What follows is a more "technical" discussion of test scores designed to assist parents in reading reports of psychological or educational testing when questions arise. This particular section of the book may not be meaningful if read without a specific purpose in mind. Therefore, it is recommended that parents skip this section unless interested in understanding available scores. If you wish to skip this section, you can go ahead to the next section entitled "What Does It All Mean?" Always, the best source of information regarding "numbers" or test scores remains the psychological examiner who completed the testing.

How Can I Understand Test Scores?

While the focus in reviewing an assessment report should be on interpretation of test results and integration of all assessment data, unfortunately the "numbers" or scores reported for various tests, particularly IQ tests, often receive the most attention. In many cases these numbers elicit anxiety, which interferes with a parent's ability to see the larger picture that represents the "whole child." Understanding test scores, how they are derived, and the limitations inherent in their use may help alleviate some of the anxiety.

Regardless of the type of test used or the purpose of testing, the first "number" derived is a "raw score." This may be the number of answers right or the number of answers wrong, depending on how the test is scored. Just being told that a child receives a score of "ten" on a test does not provide any useful information about the child's performance. Does this mean ten of ten correct? Does this mean ten of one-hundred correct? Does this mean ten wrong? In other words, the "raw score" must be reported in a manner that gives it meaning.

Test scores are often first received in school settings where teachers and schools attempt to provide parents with feedback regarding their child's school performance. Classroom tests may be informal where teachers indicate in their own way how scoring was accomplished. Increasingly, public and private schools are instituting a more formal type measure for use in gauging classroom performance of all their students. For example, Tommy's (case #1) teacher regularly gives tests to her students to assess their progress in mastering skills. Tommy has consistently performed below expected as compared to his classmates. His teacher points out to his parents, based on test results, that Tommy has not mastered basic addition and subtraction facts, cannot tell time to the hour, and does not consistently identify monetary values of coins. Tommy's teacher is utilizing criterion-referenced tests that are specifically designed to measure certain "criteria," which in this case are the goals and objectives of second-grade math at Tommy's school.

Rather than reporting "raw scores," results from testing are usually interpreted to parents in reference to what was expected. For example, Tommy's actual score on the test used to measure math learned was 40 percent. This number does not relate anything about Tommy's general skills or knowledge in math. Tommy was expected to show mastery of ten objectives, but he only demonstrated mastery of four. This was determined by looking at Tommy's test performance on the items used to gauge mastery of each objective. These tests are usually referred to as "criterion-referenced," as performance is presented relative to preset criteria, not in comparison to other students.

"Competency" tests are now being used in many states to measure student's mastery of basic skills in reading, math, or written language prior to graduation from high school. These are "criterion-referenced" tests, also. Usually a specific score is set as the cutoff for demonstrating mastery of the skill measured. Students who do not "pass" may be required to retake the test until they achieve an acceptable score, often with special tutorial courses offered to assist in skill development.

Whether or not a student has mastered specific objectives in content areas such as math will not address other important referral questions. Often the questions to be answered inherently require comparisons to others. For example, Lisa's (case #2) parents want to know if her development is "normal," implying some form of comparison to other three-year-old children. Jeremy's (case #5) parents want to know if he is "gifted" prior to making a school placement decision. Therefore, he must be compared to other four-and-a-half-year-olds with regard to his intellectual ability. In other situations, such as Tommy's, it may be important to determine ability levels in order to set expectations adequately. For example, Tommy's teacher and principal are interested in whether he is learning at a level consistent with others his age and, also, if his learning is consistent with his general ability to learn. In other words, they wish to obtain an estimate of Tommy's ability to learn, as compared to other "average" eight-year-olds, not just to his fellow classmates. They also wish to know how much math he has learned as compared to other "average" eight-year-olds. "Norm-referenced" tests may answer these kinds of questions. They yield scores that are based on comparisons to a group, usually of the same age or grade. Formal psychological and educational tests are norm-referenced.

Norms. After a test is administered, a raw score or number of items correct is obtained. But what does Tommy's (case #1) raw score of six on a test of math calculation really mean? If the test was norm-referenced, Tommy's raw score of six may be compared to the performance of the norm group or sample of students who took the test initially in order to establish expected performance levels for age or grade. For example, as compared to other eight-year-olds, Tommy's score of six may fall below expected or below the average eight-year-old in the "normative sample."

The appropriateness of the norm groups for use in comparisons should be apparent. For many psychological and educational tests, the norm group is selected to provide a representative sample of the population in the United States within the age range for which the test is designed. Factors considered include grade level, gender, socioeconomic status, geographic region, and ethnicity. Some tests are constructed to provide comparisons to a specific segment of the population such as individuals with sensory handicaps (deaf or visually impaired). Other important considerations include the size of the sample at each age/grade level included and date the norms were established.

Specification of the norm group used to evaluate an examinee's performance may be important. For example, evaluation of a Hispanic child without adequate mastery of English using norms based on English speaking children from the majority culture in the United States must proceed with caution. If the purpose of testing is to predict success in the majority culture, there may be some value in these comparisons. However, statements about the Hispanic child's ability level based on these norms would be inappropriate.

Scores based on comparisons to norms are called *derived scores*. This means that the obtained or raw score was transformed into units that allow comparisons to similar others as well as comparison of different scores earned by the same individual. The procedure is similar to converting all measures for building a house to the same standard — feet or metric — instead of mixing the two. This allows easy comparison of units of measurement. The most commonly used derived scores are age- and grade-equivalents, percentile ranks, and standard scores. However, they vary according to usefulness in interpreting test performance.

Results from norm-referenced tests designed to answer the questions posed by Tommy's (case #1) teacher and principal will be used to help illustrate the derived scores. The Woodcock-Johnson-Revised, Tests of Achievement (WJ-R) consists of subtests measuring achievement levels in basic academic skill areas that yield "clusters" or global indices in each area.

Woodcock-Johnson-Revised, Tests of Achievement (WJ-R)

Cluster	Age Equivalent	Grade Equivalent
Broad Mathematics	6–11	1.5
Broad Reading	9–1	3.8
Broad Written Language	8–8	3.3

Age- and grade-equivalents. Look at Tommy's age- and grade-equivalent scores in mathematics, reading, and written language. The age equivalent of six years eleven months in mathematics means that Tommy's performance in the Broad Mathematics cluster of the WJ-R was most similar to that of children six years eleven months of age who were included in the normative sample. Grade equivalents are interpreted similarly. Tommy's grade equivalent of 1.5 in the Broad Mathematics cluster means that his performance was similar to that of children in the fifth month of first grade in comparison to the norm sample for his age.

Age- and grade-equivalents allow consideration of a child's test performance in a developmental context. That is, they give general information regarding whether a child is ahead, behind, or on par with others of the same age or grade. This is important to remember as all too often these scores are interpreted literally. For example, "Tommy's functioning at the nine year, one month level in reading, according to achievement test results, and is only eight years old!" is an overgeneralization. These test results suggest that Tommy is functioning above average in age comparisons; not that he has the reading ability of a nine year, one month old.

Caution is necessary in using grade equivalents for a number of reasons. They reflect comparisons to the norm group, not to peers at a particular school, and thus, may be misleading. For example, formal testing in reading shows that Tommy (case #1) is reading on a 3.8 grade level (eighth month of third grade), but this may be well below the expected level for his second-grade classmates in a private school setting. Similarly, comparisons using age or grade equivalents across tests, and even across subtests within a test, are unwarranted since they are not based on solid numerical scales that reflect consistency in score differences.

When relative differences, both in comparisons to peers and with regard to a child's own pattern or "profile" of strengths and weaknesses is desired, other types of scores prove more useful than age- and grade-equivalents. These include percentile ranks and various types of standard scores.

Woodcock-Johnson-Revised, Tests of Achievement (WJ-R)

Cluster	Percentile Rank for Age
Broad Mathematics	9
Broad Reading	89
Broad Written Language	74

Percentile Ranks. Percentile ranks or scores offer another means of comparing how a child performs with other students who took the test (those in the norm or comparison group). The range of possible scores falls between 0.1 and 99.9. It is not possible to have percentile ranks of 0 or 100. Interpretation of percentile ranks is based on the percentage of *people*, not percentage of correct scores. For example, Tommy's percentile rank of 89 in the WJ-R Broad Reading cluster means that the obtained raw score was as good as or better than scores for 89 percent of the age comparison group for that test. More specifically, Tommy's raw score in reading suggests that he performed as well as or better than 89 percent of the group of eight-year-olds to whom he was compared.

When scores are reported for norm-referenced tests,

percentile ranks should be included for all appropriately administered norm-referenced tests, as they are the most useful to parents and teachers in describing a child's performance. For example, it is easily apparent that Tommy's WJ-R math performance falls significantly below average, as the ninth percentile is far below the fiftieth percentile, while reading and written language are above average. Also, it is possible to compare a child's performance across different tests or across "subtests" within the same test by using percentiles. In looking at the results from the WJ-R for Tommy, analysis of percentiles for each of the clusters reveals a gap between Tommy's Broad Mathematics percentile of 9 as compared to his Broad Reading percentile of 89 and Broad Written Language percentile rank of 74. This difference can be interpreted to reveal that as measured by the WJ-R math achievement falls significantly below achievement in reading and written language. This process of comparing scores to assess for strengths and weaknesses is referred to as profile analysis.

Woodcock-Johnson — Revised, Tests of Achievement (WJ-R)

Cluster	Standard Scores (Mean=100; Standard Deviation=15)
Broad Mathematics	80
Broad Reading	118
Broad Written Language	110

Standard Scores. Standard scores are derived by converting a raw score to a scale chosen by the test developer. Just as a surveyor may measure roads in miles or kilometers, and convert with confidence from one to the other, test developers select their own scale. When reviewing standard scores derived from any administration of a norm-referenced test, you need to know the scale chosen by the test developer.

Standard score scales are defined by two parameters — the "mean" or average scale and the standard deviation. Together, the mean and standard deviation may be used to help determine how far an individual's own standard score lies from average in comparison to the norm group. In testing, the standard deviation is the standard used to gauge how far above or below the mean a score falls. Thus, we can compare test results across subtests or tests by comparing how many standard deviations above or below the mean a score falls, even when different tests are used.

Consider Tommy's (case #1) standard scores from the WJ-R. His standard score of 80 in mathematics falls more than one standard deviation below the average or mean score of 100 or more than 15 points below 100. In contrast, Tommy's reading standard score falls more than one standard deviation (more than 15 points) above the average or mean score of 100.

The majority of norm-referenced or standardized tests used by psychologists employ the scale where 100 is the mean or average and the standard deviation is 15. Other types of standard scores may infrequently be encountered in reading psychological reports. A T-score has a mean of 50 and a standard deviation of 10, for example. Some college entrance examinations or professional certifying exams have selected a scale where 500 is considered average and the standard deviation is set at 100. Test developers may establish their own scale to help distinguish their test from others, or to distinguish composite and subtest scores. For example, the most commonly used tests of intelligence, the Wechsler scales, use different standard scores for IQs and subtests. Below are Tommy's scores from the Wechsler Intelligence Scale for Children-Revised (WISC-R) to illustrate this point.

Wechsler Intelligence Scale for Children-Revised (WISC-R)

Full Scale IQ 115

Verbal IQ	114	Performance IQ	112
	Scale		Scale
Verbal Subtests	Scores	Performance Subtests	Scores
Information	13	Picture Completion	13
Similarities	14	Picture Arrangement	14
Arithmetic	8	Block Design	12
Vocabulary	13	Object Assembly	7
Comprehension	14	Coding	13
(Digit Span)	(11)	(Mazes)	(7)

In order to make sense of the WISC-R results we must know the scales chosen by the test developer. For the IQs, the mean is 100 and the standard deviation 15, just as in the WJ-R and many other psychological and educational tests. The *subtest* scale scores are on a scale where 10 is considered average and the standard deviation is 3. Tommy's scores can be interpreted with regard to the mean. For example, his Full Scale IQ is one standard deviation above the mean, or 15 points above 100.

Similarly, Tommy scored at least one standard deviation (3 points) above the average or mean of 10 on several subtests. Thus, even though the subtest and IQ scores are on different scales, they may be interpreted similarly. It is possible to convert from one standard score to another, just as a builder or surveyor might convert from inches to feet to yards in measuring length.

When the mean and standard deviation of different tests used are the same, comparisons of obtained standard scores can easily be made. To illustrate, let's return to Tommy (case #1) and compare scores obtained. Results from a standardized intelligence test with a mean of 100 and a standard deviation of 15 yielded a global IQ score of 115, which is high average in norm group comparisons to others his age. However, his standard score on the Broad Math area of the Woodcock-Johnson-Revised Tests of Achievement (WJ-R), where the mean is also 100 and the standard deviation 15, was 80. When these two scores are compared, Tommy's score in math achievement may be interpreted as falling more than two standard deviations below his IQ or estimated general ability level. Thus, Tommy's measured achievement in math is much lower than expected given the obtained estimate of his intellectual ability.

It is generally accepted that differences of one standard deviation or more between two standard scores, where they are from the same scale (that is, one where the mean and standard deviation used were the same), should be considered to reflect some real difference in the abilities measured. These differences can be in comparison within a test or across tests. For example, Tommy's measured achievement in reading in the WJ-R, where the obtained standard score is 118, can be compared to his math achievement standard score of 80. The interpretation is that his measured reading achievement is more than two standard deviations above his measured math achievement.

Unreliability of Test Scores. Caution must be exercised when making standard score comparisons because all tests are not equally reliable (see chapter 2). This means that test scores obtained on one occasion may be different when the test is repeated later. Scores may be higher or lower the second time. For example, Tommy, who got a 115, may be retested in one year with the same IQ test and obtain a Full Scale IQ of 120. His parents may be delighted. However, this does not mean that Tommy has "gained intelligence." The first IQ score of 115 should actually be considered an estimate, because of the unreliability of the test. "True" scores can never be ascertained as no perfectly reliable tests exist. Thus, all scores on norm-referenced tests are actually estimates.

Test unreliability should be considered to prevent misinterpretation and misuse of test results. This becomes particularly important in two situations — in re-evaluations and in using test scores to make selection or placement decisions. For example, Allison (case #7) was retested on the same IQ test that was administered previously. Her previous IQ was 52. She obtained an IQ of 60 in retesting. However, the psychologist explained to her parents that the second score should not be considered to reflect "real" gains in intellectual functioning. Rather unreliability in the first test score was high.

Comparing test results to preset "cutoff" scores fails to take into consideration the unreliability of tests. In Jeremy's case (#5), he was tested on the Wechsler Preschool and Primary Scale of Intelligence-Revised (WPPSI-R) to ascertain his eligibility for a program for gifted children. The cutoff score set by the school was

130. Jeremy obtained a score of 128. When the psychologist interpreted this score to Jeremy's parents he referred to the unreliability of the score, which suggested that it should not be used as an absolute. Specifically the psychologist referred to the Standard Error of Measurement (SEM) (calculated when the test is developed by the developer) that is used to reflect the unreliability of test scores. The SEM for this test at Jeremy's age is 4. Thus, Jeremy's "true" IQ was estimated to fall somewhere between 124 and 132, given the unreliability of the test. The psychologist recommended that Jeremy be accepted in the gifted program, in consideration of all data gathered during the assessment process. Adherence to the cutoff score by the school would fail to take into account the unreliability of the test as well as the professional opinion of the psychologist that is based on a broad assessment, not just one test.

When parents are unclear what an increase or decrease in scores means, they should ask, and continue to ask, until they receive an answer they understand. Also, parents may wish to ask about the reliability of tests employed where decisions are based on cutoff scores before entering the selection process.

What Does It All Mean?

Interpretation of psychological test data may be reported in a test-by-test manner or by "domain" or area of functioning (e.g., motor ability, auditory processing, visual-spatial processing, language, memory, etc.). A clear statement reflecting interpretation of test data in each area or test should characterize the child's functioning. Inconsistencies in test data should be explored in the report. Clinical impressions or hypotheses regarding the reasons for the inconsistencies should be clearly noted.

Parents should expect a clear interpretation of the test data in consideration of all other sources of information — the child's background, attitude, and temperament; observed behavior; interviews; and any other background information. This interpretation should then support the presentation of hypotheses or clinical and diagnostic impressions regarding the meaning of all assessment results. These will not be "firm" causal statements since psychological assessment cannot firmly establish cause. Behavior is influenced by far too many factors in far too complex a fashion to be able to predict with 100 percent accuracy what process leads to what behavior. Rather, test results allow speculation with regard to underlying psychological processes and their impact on the individual.

"Diagnoses." Consistency in assessment results provides a basis for the impressions and comparisons to diagnostic criteria used in the formulation of diagnoses. There are no single tests available for any particular diagnostic category. For example, mental deficiency is not diagnosed based only on measured intelligence, although significantly below average intelligence is an integral part of the diagnostic criteria. Additional tests of adaptive behaviors or functions, as well as consideration of other information gained through assessment, must be interpreted together to formulate an impression regarding mental deficiency. Tests do not lead to diagnoses. Rather an assessment process, which may or may not include formal testing, provides the basis for formulation of diag-

noses. Furthermore, diagnoses will not always be offered in psychological test reports. They are provided only as needed to address the referral question(s).

Diagnostic impressions are often reported in formats from two standard sources. In addition to diagnostic area names (e.g., Mental Retardation, Enuresis, Attention Deficit Hyperactivity Disorder) numeric codes used for insurance-filing purposes and record keeping in many clinical or hospital settings are also used. Psychologists most frequently utilize the *Diagnostic and Statistical Manual*, 3rd Edition, Revised (*DSM-III-R*) of the American Psychiatric Association. Another classification system used by physicians, may also be used by psychologists — the *International Classification of Diseases*, 9th Revision, published by the World Health Organization. The *DSM-III-R*, scheduled to be updated to *DSM-IV* in the early 1990s, reflects the current criteria utilized to establish a diagnosis. As in other data contained in reports, parents should inquire as to the meaning of the diagnoses or ask for specification of the criteria for making the diagnoses.

Often psychological testing is completed for school-placement purposes. In those cases, the report should refer to the classification system used by schools for decision making for special education placement if a clear indication for eligibility is apparent. This would include reference to categories included in PL 94-142 (Individuals with Disabilities Educational Act — formerly the Education of All Handicapped Children Act), such as mentally retarded, learning disabled, or gifted. Specific information may be needed, such as the level of mental retardation, the type of learning disability (e.g., reading comprehension or math calculation), or the type of "gift-edness" (e.g., intellectual or creative talent). To further confuse matters, each state, and even jurisdictions within states may vary somewhat in the criteria used for eligibility, the specific terminology accepted, and the procedures for accepting testing done outside the school. If testing is being completed for possible school placement decision, the psychologist should be knowledgeable so that the report may be written accordingly.

Something that often confuses parents further is that diagnoses applied by psychologists based on *DSM-III-R* do not easily match the labels applied by school systems in placing children in special programs. For example, after an evaluation, Brad (case #6) might be diagnosed with Oppositional Disorder. However, the school system would probably classify him as Emotionally Disturbed for placement purposes. Tommy (case #1) might be given a *DSM-III-R* diagnosis of Developmental Arithmetic Disorder, but the school system would call him Learning Disabled. For Brian (case #8), a psychologist may diagnose him as experiencing Major Depression, or Conduct Disorder, but there may be no corresponding label in the school system because they have no special placement for him. This would be especially true if Brian's grades were passing.

Parents may need to sit down with the psychologist who did the testing to review the findings and particularly any diagnostic comments or opinions. Making sure that the results from the psychological testing can be translated into a language that the school system uses in determining placement will be very important in facilitating use of test results for educational placement.

Recommendations. A parent should expect more than a diagnostic label from a report. There should be an approach to intervention clearly based on the child's overall performance, including strengths and weaknesses. These should be presented in a clear manner, including goals and treatment strategies. It is helpful to have the recommendations listed in order of priority or in sequence if one treatment approach or strategy may be contingent on another. Also, parents should expect guidance in finding referral sources for obtaining recommended interventions or additional testing. The reasons for follow-up testing, if suggested, should be clear.

Many parents may be frustrated by the failure of psychological assessment to clearly explain "cause" or predict behavior. The "videotape" of a child, provided by the parent through interview, history taking, record sharing, and anecdotes can help the psychologist approximate a picture of the "whole child." However, specific human behaviors and personality attributes are too complex to be directly associated with single causal factors. Rather biological and environmental factors must be considered along with the cognitive and behavioral aspects of a child's functioning. Similarly, prediction based on psychological assessment is difficult. Behavior and cognitive functioning will be influenced by biological and environmental changes that are impossible to predict clearly. Cautious predictions are possible; however, long-range predictions are generally avoided to protect the child. They may lead to unrealistic expectations, either too high or too low, which may potentially harm the child. A better plan, particularly when a problem has been noted, is to recheck functioning at each successive stage of development or more often if problems continue.

Reporting Results to Children and Adolescents

Although children rarely come for help of their own voli-tion and rarely are the problems they have theirs alone, it is important that they become part of the assessment pro-cess aimed at "solving" the presenting problem(s). They should be part of the efforts directed toward discovering the causes of the difficulties. Interpreting the results of the tests to them in a language they can understand can help mobilize them as part of the decision-making and treatment-planning process if treatment is indicated.

How the interpretation of the test results to the child takes place is determined by the relationship between the examiner, the referral source, and the parent. Sometimes the referring person may be a mental health professional who is seeing the child and/or family. Even though this individual did not do the testing, he or she may know how to present the results in such a way as to facilitate the helping process. If there are any specific questions regarding the tests they will often suggest talking with the examiner.

More often than not, the psychologist who adminis-tered the tests does the interpretation with the child since he or she is most acquainted with the test findings. This is done by some examiners with the child in an individ-ual session. It also may be done with the parents and child together, depending on the examiner's customary procedure, the examiner's view of what would be best, and the parent's wishes. Sometimes the child is seen for the interpretive session prior to the parents; sometimes later.

It is important that the interpretation of psychological test data be completed by someone familiar with the tests and the results. For that reason, we suggest it not be done by any person who has limited knowledge of testing or limited knowledge of the child and family.

In interpreting the test results to the child it is important also that it be done in a manner that can be understood by the child. The child should be encouraged to ask questions. Sensitivity is required as test results are often used as the basis for decision making and the child may be "painfully" aware of the implications of his or her performance. For example, when testing is used to determine if a child should be placed in a class for gifted students and the examiner feels that such a placement is not wise, the child has to be encouraged to recognize that he or she has many talents and skills that can be fostered and developed in regular settings. The parents will also need help in recognizing that, to be successful, a child does not have to be in a "gifted" program. Thus testing becomes part of a process of discovery and planning for all.

Caution must be exerted in reporting results to children and adolescents. In general, an explanation for the testing should be given at the outset. Usually something such as "the tests will help us find out what you do best and to discover those areas where you may be having problems." If such a preliminary statement was used, then reporting results should follow similar lines. Statements about strengths, with less emphasis on problem areas, should be given.

It is recommended that children and adolescents up to the age of eighteen not be allowed to read the report. Rather, they should be given an oral report of test results.

When There Is No Clear Answer, What Should I Do?

Often results of psychological assessment yield several hypotheses regarding the presenting problems. This may result in recommendations for either further testing or treatment, to be followed by testing, to establish its efficacy. When this is the case, parents should attempt to gain a clear understanding of what the psychologist is recommending. A specific treatment and assessment plan may be part of the report. Follow-up phone calls to clarify steps in the treatment and assessment process should be made, as needed.

In other cases, a parent may be dissatisfied or disagree with results. Consultation, where test data is reviewed by another professional, may help in such a situation.

8

What If I Disagree?

I did these things at that other lady's office and I already told her what they are!
— Sixteen-year-old being reevaluated

PSYCHOLOGICAL testing has been completed and you have an oral and/or written report of the results and recommendations. Some of the words used may have been unclear or technical, so you have used the glossary of this book to understand them. However, after thinking about what was said, you disagree with the conclusions and feel that certain factors were not adequately addressed, certain significant information overlooked, or certain statements not entirely accurate. You also have questions about the recommendations, as in the case of Jeremy (#5). He was evaluated as not ready for kindergarten, but his parents felt he was not well on the day of testing and therefore did not perform at his optimal level.

You have a right to an explanation of what you do not understand. It is most appropriate to discuss your concerns first with the psychologist who did the testing. If you are not satisfied with the result of that discussion, you may wish to have another psychologist or the referring person look over the report and talk with them about your concerns. Remember, psychological testing does not stand on its own, but requires interpretation to be meaningful. Thus, a report will always have interpretations, opinions, and may even have speculations.

Psychology, as other young fields, is not an exact science. This is a point we have mentioned several times throughout this book. As a result, different professionals in the field will have different philosophies, approaches, and beliefs about the meaning of test data or behavior, and different ideas about intervention. Take the case of Edward (#10) described earlier. This boy's dog, a cherished family pet, died. Edward seems to be having difficulty grieving. Suppose that during the interview process, he described his father as a giant of a man who could do no wrong and would make everything right. A statement or description of this kind alone could have at least two different interpretations. One would be that Edward perceives his father as larger than life. Another would be that he wishes his father was this way, perhaps so he could bring back the family dog. Suppose further that upon meeting Edward's father, the psychologist discovers him to be short of stature, quiet, and usually deferring to Edward's mother during the interview. Does the interpretation change?

The point here is that most psychologists believe what children talk about, imagine, cry about, etc., has some importance. Despite the reality, it is the psychologist's job to try to discover, through tests, interviews, observations, and background information, what it all means. Integrating all of the information as thoroughly and carefully as possible is necessary. Still, this will not guarantee that another psychologist would see everything the same way, or that you as the parent would see it the same.

In these cases, it is important that the atmosphere be open and honest so that a parent's thoughts about his or her child and family can be discussed with the evaluator. Yet, if after discussing the results with your friends, relatives, other professionals, and/or the person who recommended testing, questions remain, parents always can seek a second opinion. In a setting such as a school where testing services are free, you very likely will need to pay for this second opinion (although there are some exceptions to this).

A publication by the Children's Defense Fund (1989) describes the procedures for testing by a school psychologist for special education services within the school system. While you clearly have more control over the entire situation if you retained the psychologist privately or independently, you still have some recourse if you disagree with a school-based evaluation. First, you need to meet with the parties involved to state your disagreements and request another evaluation. If the school personnel agree, the decision is whether it should be independent or within the school system. Most of the time it would be an independent evaluation that is recommended. If the school disagrees, you have a right to a hearing where a board would decide whether another evaluation is appropriate. If the board decides it is appropriate, the school will pay. If not, there will be no funding.

It is generally recommended that parents pursue the independent evaluation on their own, then request that the school reimburse them for the evaluation if the board agrees that the evaluation was warranted. This saves time, gets the process moving, and often the results will be helpful at any hearings. There is *No guarantee*, however, that the school board would reimburse parents for such an expense. In general (for good fiscal reasons), school systems would prefer to use their own staff for all evaluations and interventions, and are resistant to funding services from private sources (see the CDF publication listed in the bibliography for a further explanation of this process).

A point to keep in mind as a parent is that you have a great deal of input into what can and cannot be in your child's school record. If you contracted initially for the independent evaluation, you get the report. Whether or not you share the report with the school is entirely up to you. Now, it is probably true that it is typically more to your advantage to share the report than not. However, if you disagree with the report, its findings, or recommendations, you do not need to release it to the school. You also can object to a school based evaluation being included in your child's records. Again, it is not as clear-cut as when you have paid for the initial evaluation. However, you can object to the report on grounds that it is inaccurate or misleading. You will most likely be asked for substantiation of such claims. Bear in mind, though, that the results of an independent evaluation are in your hands.

If you decide that either a second or an independent evaluation is necessary, it is important that you tell the psychologist what concerns you have and give him or her permission to obtain any necessary test results from the first psychologist rather than attempt to relate them yourself. The materials in psychological tests frequently contain easily recognizable phrases or statements. These can be misinterpreted when taken out of context, or when reviewed by someone not trained in doing psychological assessments. Therefore, it is critical that the raw materials (raw data) from psychological tests be shared only with another trained psychologist who is familiar with the tests and who has experience testing children.

In selecting a psychologist for a second or independent opinion, his or her qualifications should be equivalent to the first psychologist's. This is good common sense and is also a requirement where the independent evaluation comes after a school-based assessment. It would not be reasonable, for example, to use a fully licensed doctoral level psychologist for the first evaluation, and a bachelor's level psychological technician for the second opinion.

Unfortunately, some tests cannot be repeated immediately because of "practice effects." Unless an adequate amount of time has passed between testings, the test questions may be so familiar as to produce invalid results. These invalid results will not necessarily mean the scores are higher or better. Sometimes if children remembered how they answered the first time they were tested, they may answer the same way again even if the answer or response is wrong. Thus, it makes it nearly impossible to interpret the data or use them to understand a child. The examiner giving the second opinion may need the original protocols. Those can be obtained only with your written permission.

Now that you have two opinions, what do you do? If they agree, it would be unlikely that you would seek a third. This is true even when it is hard to accept the results or recommendations. If the two reports disagree, then you have a number of options:

1. You have to decide whether to seek still another opinion.

2. You will have to choose the one that feels most accurate to you and begin to implement the recommendations.

3. You will have to initiate some of the recommendations and see if they help after a certain period of time. Remember that in carrying out the recommendations there may be many ups and downs, slow and fast times, advances and setbacks, steps forward and backward. Most of the time the decisions made on the basis of testing are not irreversible. Thus, if you have started on a particular path that has not been successful you can always change, and find someone else to help you or ask for a reevaluation after a period of time.

The idea of reevaluation after a period of time is essential to the planning and treatment process. Parents often are unsure of decisions even when great care has been taken in making them. Frequently, the only way to know if something will be helpful or effective is to try it and see. Supposing that Jeremy (case #5) was evaluated and found not to fall in the "gifted" range by one psychologist, but was thought to be gifted by another. His parents could start him in a program for gifted children and keep a close eye on how he does, the amount of stress he feels, how he handles that pressure, how much he enjoys the program, etc. They could also ask for a reevaluation to make sure he is in an appropriate school setting. Conversely, they could decide to let him go into a regular kindergarten class and also keep a close eye on how he does, the amount of stress he feels, how he handles it, and how he enjoys the program. Again, they could reevaluate him and see if he is better prepared to handle an advanced program or whether he should stay where he is.

Many of the cases from chapter 1 lend themselves to illustrating the need for a second opinion. An example of dealing with a second opinion could be with Brad (case #6). Brad's mother gave permission for the school to conduct psychological testing, despite the fact that she did not agree that he was having severe problems. She did not see problems at home and believed the teachers were not strict enough with him. Suppose the school psychologist conducts an evaluation and finds that Brad is emotionally disturbed. As a result of this evaluation, the school system is recommending placement in a special school for emotionally disturbed children some distance from Brad's home.

What responses or actions can Brad's mother take? Given that she did not believe there were serious problems to start with, she is not likely to agree fully with such test findings. She can request another evaluation be done through the school system, although an independent evaluation might provide a more objective point of view. She could also look to retain an independent psychologist, either someone in private practice or through the community mental-health center (where services are often provided on a sliding fee scale). If the results concur with those of the school system, Brad's mother can either agree with the placement decision or appeal it. An appeal, though, will be hard to support with two evaluations suggesting that Brad needs special attention.

If the independent evaluator does not believe that Brad is emotionally disturbed, but is reacting to something that is transient in his life, and could be maintained in a regular classroom with some behavioral contracts, the stage is set for discussion and negotiation with the school system. This could lead to a hearing through the school system's appeal process where a board hears the arguments on both sides and then decides what they believe is best for the child. However, if the independent evaluation is well done and convincing, the decision could be made at a program level for an attempt at a particular level of intervention to see what can be done to help Brad control himself better in school and learn the needed materials.

As can be seen, often the only test for whether an evaluation is accurate or not is to initiate an intervention and then reevaluate at some point later. If progress is made, then the program and intervention can remain. If not, then some changes will need to be made. For example, supposing that the school system concurs with the independent evaluation recommendation to keep Brad in his current classroom with behavior contracts (agreements regarding rewards for appropriate behavior). However, after six months Brad's behavior has not improved and in fact is somewhat worse. This would begin to imply that perhaps Brad does need more intense intervention and programming available through the program for emotionally disturbed children. In this scenario, a transfer would be advised.

Another case exemplifies parents' use of a second opinion when the first professional's opinion did not allay their concerns. Lisa (case #3) was becoming a bit of a concern to her day care providers, and her parents too wondered about some of her development and her behavior. However, their pediatrician's opinion was that her behavior was within the wide range of expectable behavior for a three-year-old and suggested the parents be patient and wait. Lisa's parents, after talking between themselves, decided that instead of waiting they would look to have their daughter evaluated by a psychologist specializing in work with young children. Their hope was that the psychologist could understand not only Lisa, but their concerns about her as well.

Parents might seek second opinions for a wide variety of reasons. School placement is probably a leading reason. Disagreements in one form or another with a school's recommendations, whether it be for self-contained classrooms with little mainstreaming (integration into nonspecial education classes for some periods a day) or vice versa, can lead to requesting a second evaluation. In all of these examples, regardless of the disagreements and differences of opinion, people involved are trying to do what is in the best interest of the child. The most important thing is that as parents, you use the information gained from a psychological evaluation and discussion with the psychologist to make an informed decision that you truly believe to be best for your child.

9

What about Confidentiality?

What are you going to tell my mom and dad?
— Eight-year-old girl at the start of testing

THE field of psychology and all those related to mental health are founded on the cornerstone of confidentiality. The knowledge that whatever a client or patient tells the therapist or evaluator is confidential and will remain so lays the groundwork for the helping relationship, which is built on trust. When there is the possibility that topics, thoughts, behaviors, or feelings brought up in therapy might be disclosed to other individuals, no one would feel free to share meaningful and intimate thoughts.

But, what exactly does confidentiality mean, and how is it different from privacy? Privacy is the Fourth Amendment right to decide what, or how much of private feelings, thoughts, or personal knowledge to share with someone. Confidentiality, on the other hand, is the professional standard of conduct that requires a practitioner not to discuss the information obtained from someone with anyone else. Confidentiality is a concept that has both ethical and legal bases. The code of ethics for psychologists mandates that psychologists not divulge information shared with them by their clients except in unique situations (where there is the potential for harm). Statute or case law, depending upon the state, provides the legal basis for the concept.

There is one other concept that has to be defined here, and that is the concept of *privilege*. This legal term refers to the protection under the law granted to certain types of relationships. Protection here means that a person cannot be forced to disclose information in any legal proceedings. Privilege belongs to, or is "held" by the client. Some legal jurisdictions extend the same privilege rights as granted to client-lawyer or patient-doctor relationships to psychologist-client relationships.

When children are the clients, parents (or other legal guardians) hold the privilege. Parents are the ones responsible for signing all release-of-information forms and inspecting school or hospital records. Therefore, in a strict legal sense, only the parents (or legal guardian) can decide what to do with the report of a psychological evaluation.

There are agreed upon limits as to how far confidentiality will extend. It is both a matter of professional ethics and of law that a psychologist cannot maintain a confidence when someone threatens the safety of either himself or herself or another person. Many states now have statutes governing this and lay out with varying degrees of clarity what a professional is to do. Most of the time it requires that the professional contact authorities, warn the intended victim, hospitalize or take steps to hospitalize the client, or in some way act to prevent the harm from occurring.

In the same way that teachers or physicians need to report suspected child abuse, psychologists need to report suspected abuse. If there is evidence of abuse, or the child discloses to the psychologist that he or she has been abused, the limits of confidentiality have been surpassed. That information cannot be kept confidential. Again, ethics and the law mandate that some action be taken to protect the child (such as reporting to the protective service agency).

There is a basic purpose to the concept of confidentiality, and that is the establishment of trust in the relationship. Confidentiality is only one way that trust is established and maintained. The creation of an atmosphere of trust is the goal of the psychologist. This extends to both the parents, and to the child. It is important to both psychological evaluations and psychotherapy that there be trust between the parents and the psychologist and the child.

In some cases — particularly when the psychologist treats everyone with respect, is genuine, and gives everyone serious consideration — people feel trust for the first time. Children may trust the psychologist more than their parents; and parents may trust the psychologist more than they do their children.

When you as a parent trust the person doing the evaluation with your child, issues of confidentiality become easier to negotiate. While in a *strict* legal sense, children are not entitled to have secrets from their parents, they would not feel free to discuss anything with a psychologist if they thought everything would be reported verbatim back to their parents. Parents who trust the evaluator will come to understand that if there was something of critical importance for them to know, they would be informed. Furthermore, parents will receive a written report describing the psychologist's observations, the test results, interpretation, and opinions regarding recommendations.

Psychologists also are very careful and thoughtful when it comes to issues of maintaining and protecting a person's privacy. For example, a psychologist might advise parents not to release certain information or evaluation reports to particular people or agencies because of the implications for the child. The psychologist, in doing that, might be considering issues such as labeling, stereotyping, or other long-term risks.

There will be a written report for parents to read and keep. You will have the opportunity in reviewing such a report together with the psychologist to ask that changes be made. While certainly the results cannot be changed, information that parents are concerned about remaining private can be discussed and often changed or removed from a report. Sometimes it is possible to have more than one report written if the report is going to different sources. For example, parents might want a comprehensive report including all observations, background, and results for their own files, but a report with a sketchier background for the school system. In these ways, parents and psychologists work together to ensure that families are protected as much as possible.

Access to Reports

It cannot be overemphasized that when using an independent psychologist, the parents are the ones who control access to the reports. It is only when other agencies become involved that this changes. For example, since Brian (case #8) is in the legal system and the court requested the evaluation, the court controls access to the report. Similarly, when foster-care systems or protective-service systems become involved and request and fund an evaluation, they control the report. However, when you as a parent seek out and retain a psychologist to evaluate your child and offer recommendations based on that evaluation, *you* control access to the report.

As parents, it is your right to decide who is able to talk with the psychologist and what the psychologist can say to other people. This must be done through a written release of information that should specify in detail what material can be released, to whom the information is going, and for what purpose. This is one method for safeguarding a family's privacy. A psychologist could not, for example, contact teachers or day-care providers to find out information about a child he or she is evaluating without the parent giving written permission for such contact.

There is a difference if the evaluation was not done by someone you retain independently. If the evaluation referral was made by a school and a school psychologist within the school system does the evaluation (after parental permission was granted), the report of results becomes part of the child's school record. As described in chapter 8, parents can contest this if they feel the report is misleading or inappropriate in some ways. There are safety features built into many school systems to protect privacy. Psychological reports are generally not kept with other information about a student, but are stored in a separate locked file. People who read those files must sign and date a log recording their use.

Even in school systems, though, parents have some control. They can refuse to allow their child to be evaluated. In our experience, this right is not frequently exercised since evaluations are typically suggested after much thought and discussion have taken place. Refusing to allow an evaluation should only be done after parents have given great care and consideration to the decision and have very good reasons why they do not want their child evaluated.

Deciding who should be allowed to see a child's test results is not always simple. Several factors should be considered in making the decision. One is the nature of the report. If the report was requested to focus on emotional or behavioral issues and the psychologist does that in the write-up, then it may not be wise to share all of that information with the school. Teachers may or may not need to know the kinds of conflicts a child is experiencing in order to be effective educators. Therefore, one issue to consider is whether or not the report and/or the information in the report is appropriate and pertinent.

Another issue to consider in making a decision about sharing a report is whether there may be a "labeling" effect. Many psychologists are very careful in their writing not to simply apply a label to a child or anyone they evaluate. However, if the report does assign a diagnosis, and you feel that it is inappropriate, or might be harmful to the child, then your decision might be not to share that particular report.

Still another issue to consider is who is asking for the information. Other professionals will often want as much information as possible from as many sources as possible to help with evaluation or treatment. Again, the question of whether the information is appropriate for the other person needs to be addressed. While often the report will be helpful to other professionals (e.g., speech therapists, occupational therapists, pediatricians, tutors, etc.), one might allay fears about sharing information by discussing with the other professionals what they will do with the report and what confidentiality they can assure within their setting. Further, a report cannot be released secondhand. That is, a tutor who has a copy of a psychological report could not release that report to a third party without written permission.

Probably the stickiest situation in psychological evaluation of children is a custody dispute. Many times parents, even the most well-meaning and best of parents, put their children in the middle of a divorce. Some of the most bitter battles are not fought over who gets the house and who the car, but who gets the children. These disputes come replete with charges of abuse made by one parent against the other, charges of neglect, and charges of being ill-fit as a parent. Often the court will order evaluations to be done. In that case, the report will go directly back to the judge or judicial magistrate. The parents will not have a say in who sees the report. Frequently, parents will retain their own psychologist who will do an evaluation separately with the hope that his or her results will favor the parent who contracted for services. In point of fact, you do not need to release the information from a report you find unfavorable to your case to the courts or professionals from the "other side," unless subpoenaed.

In the best of all possible worlds, the information from a psychological evaluation would be shared with all parties involved in the care and raising of a child. Children need support and understanding, as well as structure and routines from their parents. If a psychological assessment and report can aid in that all important process, then sharing it should benefit the child.

Alternatives to releasing a complete psychological report should always be considered. There are times when a letter from the evaluator will accomplish what is necessary. Other times, a phone conversation will suffice. The point here, though, is that parents need to think over whom to give a report, discuss any questions they have with the psychologist who did the testing, and consider all options to the report's release. The goal is to balance a family's own need for privacy with ensuring the best possible services and interventions for the child.

10

Where Do We Go from Here?

Are we done yet?
— Eight-year-old boy referred
because of oppositional behavior

Now that psychological testing has been completed and recommendations made, the next step in the process is what is to be done. In chapter 1 we presented ten cases in which psychological testing was suggested to understand the child in order to be better able to make certain decisions. What did testing show in each case, and what were the decisions that were made on the basis of the test results?

Tommy (case #1) was found to have a learning disability. It would be important for him to receive resource help. It is possible that his school (a well-known private school) is too challenging and that in order to receive the help he needs he may have to change schools. His parents might begin by trying tutoring and monitoring his progress before changing schools. A next level of intervention would be resource room help with math instead of his regular math class.

Lisa (case #2), in testing showed a general delay. Since she is very young, one would want to watch her to determine whether or not there is a deficit that would impair her performance later. An attempt might be made to intervene with occupational therapy and a speech-and-language evaluation would also be helpful. Suggestions might be made to her mother to help with Lisa's problems in separation. For example, use of some object that Lisa could literally hold onto while her mother was gone (e.g., picture, handkerchief, etc.) might be helpful. Making sure Lisa was told in language *that she could understand* (remember a referral for a speech/language evaluation was made) when her mother would be coming back might make separation easier. It would be appropriate to retest at regular intervals to watch Lisa's development over time to decide whether or not more active intervention is necessary.

Kelly (case #3) scored very high on intelligence tests. Her personality tests, however, suggested that she was working very hard at being supergood academically and socially. It was recommended that she have a diagnostic interview with serious consideration given to starting play therapy. The opinion here was that Kelly was working so hard to be perfect and holding in anything that might make her look "bad," that her stomach literally ached from it. A therapy that helped her to see herself in a realistic light and perhaps express her feelings about her family and loss of a relationship with her father could be helpful.

Because no one told the school about the severe trauma José (case #4) experienced in El Salvador, the initial findings from the evaluation considered him to be a child with an attention deficit disorder. The report recommended a trial of medication, such as Ritalin. After the dosage had been consistently increased with no change in his behavior, further investigation was completed. When a full evaluation was done (including behavior observations) it was found that José had a post-traumatic stress disorder and needed psychotherapy if his concentration was to improve. He was still dealing with the horrors and fears of living in an environment fraught with danger, where life was in a delicate balance. Therapy that would help him stop reliving the inhumanity he experienced could help him attend more in school and begin to realize his potential.

The school rejected Jeremy (case #5) for the gifted and talented class despite all indications that he was bright because his score on the IQ test was 128, two points lower than the cutoff score of 130. The school was willing to consider the error in measurement that could have placed Jeremy just as easily at 130. His parents, as noted, also explained that Jeremy wasn't feeling up to par on the day of the evaluation. Recognizing that the tests have a margin of error, Jeremy's parents appealed and Jeremy was accepted. At the end of the year, all signs seemed to indicate that Jeremy was thriving in the challenging atmosphere and thoroughly enjoyed school.

Brad (case #6) received a thorough evaluation including language and memory assessments and was found to be a seriously emotionally disturbed child whose school performance was markedly affected by his emotional condition. He therefore qualified for a meeting of the local school committee designated to rule on the eligibility status of students considered for special education. In some states, these are called Admission, Review, and Dismissal (ARD) meetings. Brad was ruled eligible for special education as an emotionally disturbed child and qualified for special services under PL 94-142. Despite serious objections from his mother, she eventually agreed to have him placed in a special class for the emotionally disturbed. Brad and his mother went to the local mental health center for therapy where his mother began to see problems at home that she had ignored.

Allison (case #7) was tested when three years old. That was not adequate to gain a picture of her current functioning. This is one of the reasons that reevaluation every three years is mandated by PL 94-142 for children in special education programs. On retesting she was found to be at the same level intellectually as earlier, but her social and adaptive skills as measured on an adaptive behavior scale were found to be higher in some areas. As a result Allison was mainstreamed at school in order to spend more time with nondisabled children doing normal activities (her peers liked her). While her cognitive/intellectual limitations would probably prevent her from pursuing college or a career requiring high academic skills, her adaptiveness will provide her with a foundation for vocational training.

Brian (case #8) was found to have done poorly in school for many years (teachers had called him an "underachiever"). His intelligence was found to be average, but he was unmotivated and resistant. There was no evidence of a learning disability. The psychological evaluation confirmed the concerns expressed by his treating psychiatrist. He was found to be extremely upset, with evidence of high suicide potential in some of the tests.

Hospitalization was strongly urged. A plan was proposed to have Brian first enter a hospital, and then a group home for adolescents while continuing in psychotherapy. The results from the psychological testing also indicated that antidepressant medication might be indicated at the present time. One last recommendation was that he be enrolled in classes at school that focused on automotives and automotive engineering.

Julie (case #9), despite a physical disability, was found to be doing well both academically and emotionally. Bright, articulate, and well adjusted, she was realistically planning for her college program, one that would prepare her to be an elementary schoolteacher. Julie needed a college that would understand her disability and be flexible and accommodate to her needs. She did not need a college that was only geared to those with physical handicaps or learning disabilities. She was able to select from a broad range of small colleges and universities with outstanding "special student services." These services would help Julie with personal attendant care (if necessary), note takers, and other aid as needed.

The evaluation of Edward (case #10), which included some personality testing and an interview, led to the recommendation of short-term counseling for his parents. While Edward may have always been a sensitive young man, there was no evidence that he was experiencing anything other than a normal, transient, though difficult grieving time. Some suggestions about the handling of grief in the family served to help everyone.

In all of these cases, children were affected in one way or another by consultation with a psychologist. Some underwent thorough batteries of tests, others had little or no testing done. For some, the testing was very helpful and important (e.g., Brian and Brad), while for others it was referral to other professionals (Lisa) that may have been most helpful. In all cases, however, the *process* of going through the evaluation, starting with the referral for testing, thinking about the child and his or her characteristics, obtaining the evaluation, and sitting down and going over the report and its recommendations served the purpose of placing the child's needs first. It focused efforts on doing what would be most helpful to the child. In that vein, the process of psychological testing, as it is combined with information from other sources, and then placed in context, plays a critical role in the life of children with difficulties.

The testing process may not always be easy to understand, and the results may not always be what parents (or psychologists) want them to be. But, taking the time to be active participants in the process, and using the information and recommendations from psychological evaluations can help parents do the best for their children.

Appendix

Tests Commonly Used
with Children and Adolescents

Following is a listing of tests that are commonly used with children and adolescents. This list is not intended to be a complete compilation of all tests that a psychologist might use with a given child. The specifics of the referral could indicate use of a test or procedure not listed here. However, the following inventory does contain those most *frequently* used by psychologists in their work with children and adolescents.

Intelligence and Other
Cognitive/Developmental Measures

Bayley Scales of Infant Development

Battell Developmental Inventory

Columbia Mental Maturity Scale

Comprehensive Evaluation of Language Functions

Detroit Tests of Learning Aptitude 2

Detroit Tests of Learning Aptitude Primary

Extended Merril-Palmer Scale

Goodenough-Harris Drawing Test

Hiskey-Nebraska Test of Learning Aptitude

Kaufman Assessment Battery for Children

Leiter International Performance Scale

McCarthy Scales of Children's Abilities

Peabody Picture Vocabulary Test-Revised

Raven's Progressive Matrices

Stanford Binet Intelligence Scale-Fourth Edition

Wechsler Preschool and Primary Scale of Intelligence-Revised

Wechsler Intelligence Scale for Children-Revised

Wechsler Intelligence Scale for Children-III (to be released in the fall, 1991)

Wechsler Adult Intelligence Scale for Children-Revised

Woodcock-Johnson-Revised Tests of Cognitive Ability

Achievement

Boehm Tests of Basic Concepts-Revised

Gray Oral Reading Test

Kaufman Tests of Educational Achievement

Keymath-Revised

Peabody Individual Achievement Test-Revised

Test of Written Language-2

Wide Range Achievement Test-Revised

Woodcock Reading Mastery Test-Revised

Woodcock-Johnson-Revised Tests of Achievement

Visual-Perceptual Measures

Bender Visual Motor Gestalt Test

Benton Visual Retention Test

Developmental Test of Visual Motor Integration

Developmental Test of Visual Perception

Purdue Perceptual Motor Survey

Test of Visual Perceptual Skills (nonmotor)

Personality/Behavior Checklists

A Comprehensive Teacher Rating Scale

Beck Depression Inventory

Child Behavior Checklist

Child Behavior Scale

Childhood Depression Inventory

Children's Apperception Test

Connors' Parent Rating Scale

Connors' Teacher Rating Scale

Devereux Adolescent Behavior Rating Scale

Devereux Child Behavior Rating Scale

House-Tree-Person Projective Drawings

Kinetic Family Drawings

Minnesota Multiphasic Personality Inventory-2

Personality Inventory for Children

Thematic Apperception Test

Rorschach

Adaptive Behavior

AAMD Adaptive Behavior Scale

Adaptive Behavior Inventory for Children

Scales of Independent Behavior

Vineland Adaptive Behavior Scales

Neuropsychological Test Batteries

Halstead-Reitan Neuropsychological Test Battery for Older Children

Luria-Nebraska Neuropsychological Battery: Children's Version

Reitan-Indiana Neuropsychological Test Battery for Children

Vocational/Career Measures

Differential Aptitude Tests

Geist Picture Interest Inventory

General Aptitude Test Battery

Strong-Campbell Interest Inventory

Wide Range Interest and Opinion Test-Revised

*Addresses and Telephone Numbers
of Important Professional Associations:*

American Psychological Association (APA)
1200 Seventeenth Street, N.W.
Washington, DC 20036
202-955-7600

American Association of State Psychology
  Boards (AASPB)
400 South Union, Suite 295
Montgomery, AL 36104
205-832-4580 or 1-800-448-4069

Council for the National Register of Health Service
  Providers in Psychology
1730 Rhode Island Ave, N.W.
Washington, DC 20036
202-833-3277

National Association of School Psychologists (NASP)
8455 Colesville Road, Suite 1000
Silver Spring, MD 20910
301-608-0500

American Board of Professional Psychology (ABPP)
2100 East Broadway, Suite 313
Columbia, MO 65201-6082
314-875-1267

Glossary

Ability Test.
An inference regarding one's capacity for performing a certain task.

Achievement.
The amount of academic material mastered.

Adaptive Behavior.
An individual's ability to cope appropriately, flexibly, and effectively with his or her environment.

Anxiety.
An emotional experience or state marked by worry, apprehension, tension, and fear.

Aphasia.
A neurological disorder characterized by an inability to understand or express words in speech, writing, or gesture.

Aptitude Test.
An inference regarding a person's ability to manifest certain skills.

Assessment.
A procedure used to evaluate an individual in terms of current functioning for diagnostic, predictive, and/or placement purposes.

Autistic Thinking.
Thinking that is primarily determined by one's personal wishes, drives, and preoccupations.

Behavioral Analysis.
A process for understanding specific observable behaviors and the observable environmental events, which elicit or inhibit those specific behaviors.

Bias.
A factor that affects objectivity and confounds test scores (other than those due to chance).

Brain Damage–MBD–Neurological Organicity.
Any anatomical or physiological change affecting the structure or foundation of the brain.

Chronological age (CA).
The number of years and months a person has lived.

Cognition.
The processes of perception, judgment, thinking, reasoning by which a person solves problems encountered in daily life.

Cognitive Style.
The unique way an individual thinks, reasons, and perceives the world.

Conduct Disorder.
A personality disorder characterized by running away, fighting, stealing, and other antisocial behaviors.

Correlation.
A statistic that represents the strength of the relationship between two measured characteristics.

Culture Fair-Test.
A test designed to reduce the influence of sociocultural background on the results.

Deciles.
Points that divide a ranked group of scores into equal tenths.

Deficit.
A loss or absence of certain functions necessary for performing certain tasks.

Developmental Disabilities.
Disabilities due to constitutional or environmental factors resulting in mental retardation, cerebral palsy, epilepsy, autism, or other problems arising during childhood.

Diagnostic Interview.
An interview designed to gather information about emotional functioning, including feelings, thoughts, and attitudes for the purpose of understanding an individual's behavior.

Diagnostic Tests.
A group of tests in a variety of areas used to assess an individual's relative strengths and weaknesses.

Down's Syndrome (Trisomy 21; Mongolism).
A congenital chromosomal defect characterized by a flat skull, thickened skin of eyelids, short fingers, and a stout body. It is usually accompanied by mental retardation, which can range from mild to severe.

DSM-III-R.
Diagnostic and Statistical Manual of Mental Disorders, Third Edition-Revised, describing the diagnostic classification system officially adopted and used by the American Psychiatric Association.

Dyslexia.
An impairment in reading or comprehending what is read.

Expressive Language Skills.
The ability to communicate ideas through speech, writing, or gesturing.

Extroversion.
A personality style characterized by tendencies toward expressiveness, social activity, and energy.

Fine Motor Skills.
The ability to perform tasks requiring small, controlled movements, such as writing, cutting with scissors, or tying knots.

Gifted.
Significantly above average IQs, or special talents in particular areas.

Grade Equivalent.
A score that represents the achievement level of the average child in the corresponding grade placement.

Gross Motor Skills.
Skills that require broad movements of the body, such as running or throwing a ball.

Group Test.
A test that can be administered to a group or class by a single person.

Hard Neurological Signs.
Evidence of brain injury that can be seen with medical technology (e.g., CT scans or MRIs).

Hyperactivity.
Unusually active behavior for a child's age, characterized by high energy, distractibility, restlessness, and short attention span.

Impulsive.
The tendency to respond or act quickly and without thinking first.

Individual Educational Program.
A unique educational plan designed for a child receiving special education services. The goal of the program is to detail and provide the services a child will need to maximize his or her educational potential.

Individual Test.
A test that was designed to be administered to only one person at a time.

Intelligence.
A person's capacity to undertake tasks characterized by abstract thinking, learning ability, and adapting to new situations.

Intelligence Quotient (IQ).

A summary score, originally developed by obtaining the ratio between mental age (MA) and chronological age (CA): $IQ = MA/CA \times 100$. Common practice now is to compute a Deviation IQ, which is the discrepancy between the person's score and the mean score for his or her age.

Interview.

A procedure for gathering information through discussion, or direct questions.

Introversion.

A personality style characterized by a tendency toward social withdrawal and reflection.

IQ.

See Intelligence Quotient.

Labeling.

Describing children using terms based on formal classification systems, such as gifted, mentally retarded, learning disabled, and emotionally disturbed.

Learning Disability.

A disorder in which there is a significant discrepancy between measured intellectual potential and actual level of school achievement that cannot be explained by emotional, environmental, or sensory impairments.

Least Restrictive Environment.

The aspect of PL 94-142 that encourages the interaction of disabled students or students receiving special education services with students in the regular classrooms.

Long-term Memory.
The storage system where individuals keep (and retrieve) information for relatively long periods of time.

Loose Association.
A thought process characterized by difficulty discussing one topic and following tangential thoughts evoked by some idea.

Mainstreaming.
The educational philosophy and practice of placing disabled children in nondisabled classroom settings with supportive special education services, such as a resource room, physical access, communication support, etc.

Maturation.
The process of psychobiological development.

Maturational Lag.
Delay in physiological, psychological, or neurological development.

MBD.
See Minimal Brain Dysfunction

Mean.
The arithmetical average found by adding up scores and dividing the total by the number of scores.

Measurement Error.
Fluctuations in a test score due to random error.

Median (MD).
The midpoint of a distribution or set of ranked scores; the score that divides the group into two equal parts; the fiftieth percentile.

Memory Span.
Number of items that can be recalled after presentation.

Mental Age (MA).
An age equivalent score that represents the thinking and reasoning of an average child of the corresponding chronological age.

Mental Deficiency.
See Mental Retardation.

Mental Retardation.
Refers to significantly below-average intellectual functioning concomitant with below-average adaptive skills for one's age. Onset is during the developmental period.

Minimal Brain Dysfunction (MBD).
A relatively mild impairment of brain functioning that is characterized by impulsive behavior, perceptual-motor difficulties, or short attention span.

Motivation.
A driving force behind behavior.

Neurological Handicap.
An impairment of the brain or central nervous system.

Neurological Lag.
Neurological development that matures at a slower pace than other physical development.

Neuropsychology.
Branch of psychology that studies brain-behavior relationships.

Nonverbal Test.
A test consisting of materials that are presented without language and that do not require the individual to respond through formal language.

Norms.
A group of scores of a known population against which an individual's performance is compared.

Objective Test.
A test that is scored by comparing the individual's responses to a list of answers determined beforehand as having particular meaning.

Organic/Organicity.
A term that refers to some sort of impairment of the brain or central nervous system.

Pathognomonic.
A single sign or symptom that *strongly* suggests the presence of a particular disorder.

Percentile Rank.
The percentage of scores that fall at or below a particular score (ranges from 1 to 99).

Perception.
The process of detecting, interpreting, and organizing sensory stimulation.

Perceptual Disorder.
An impairment in the ability to recognize, discriminate, or integrate information seen, heard, or touched.

Perceptual Motor.
A term describing the interaction of vision, hearing, or touch with motor activity.

Performance Test.
A test that minimizes the role of language and typically requires an individual to respond behaviorally in some manner.

Perseveration.
The inability to stop responding in a certain manner, regardless of whether it is appropriate or not.

PL 94-142.
The Individuals with Disabilities Educational Act, the public law that mandated public education for disabled children in the least-restrictive environment.

PL 99-457.
Amendments to PL 94-142 that extend the mandate for public special education to newborns, infants, and toddlers.

Placement.
The assigning of children to one or more specific instructional or treatment settings that are believed to be most appropriate.

Profile.
The graphic representation of results from several tests (or subtests) after the results have been transformed to some standard terms (e.g., standard scores, percentile ranks, or grade equivalents).

Projective Technique.
A method of personality assessment that presents am-

biguous stimuli to an individual with the assumption that his or her interpretation reflects inner needs, feelings, experiences, thoughts, etc.

Psychoeducational Diagnostician.
A specialist who evaluates a child who is having difficulty learning across a wide variety of tasks to specify exactly the nature of the child's problem.

Psychological Test.
A systematic procedure for measuring human characteristics that relate to observable and internal behavior.

Psychometrics.
The measurement of psychological constructs, such as intelligence, aptitude, and emotional disturbance. Also, the statistical design and property of psychological tests.

Psychomotor.
Motor behavior that either has a psychological component (e.g., sensory/motor coordination) or is influenced by psychological processes.

Psychosis (Childhood Psychosis).
A severe psychological disorder characterized by a disturbance in perception, social relationships, language, motor behavior, and emotional processes.

Quartiles.
Points that divide a ranked group of scores into equal fourths.

Questionnaire.
A list of questions concerning a particular topic, ad-

ministered to an individual to gather information about their preferences, beliefs, interests, or behavior.

Rapport.
A sense of comfort and trust in a relationship.

Raw Score.
An examinee's obtained score on a test (usually the number correct).

Readiness Test.
A test that measures the extent to which an individual has developed the foundation skills necessary for learning a more complex subject such as reading.

Receptive Language.
The ability to comprehend what is being communicated, either orally, visually, or graphically.

Reliability.
The degree to which a test obtains accurate and consistent results.

Remediation.
Intervention, usually in addition to regular instruction or treatment, designed to increase skills that are slower in developing.

Reversal.
Printing or writing letters backwards, or transposing letters in a word (e.g., *was* for *saw*).

Rigidity.
Difficulty changing an attitude or approach to problem solving even when such an approach is no longer successful or appropriate.

School Phobia.
A term that previously was used to describe a child with a specific fear of attending school. Currently, such a child would be diagnosed with an anxiety disorder, with the various features described.

Selection.
The process of choosing applicants for a program, usually based on test data or other information.

Self-concept.
A person's belief about his or her own identity, skills, attitudes, or capabilities.

Self-Report Inventory.
A personality or interest test consisting of a list of descriptions that the individual rates as being characteristic or not characteristic of himself or herself.

Sensorimotor.
Combination of the input of sense organs and the output of motor activity.

Separation Anxiety.
A fear experienced when an individual (usually a child) is separated from someone to whom he or she is very attached, typically the parent or caregiver.

Short-term Memory.
The temporary storage of information.

Significant Difference.
A discrepancy between two numbers/scores that is of such a magnitude that the probability that the difference was random is very low.

Social Quotient (SQ).
An index of a person's ability to function independently and take responsibility for his or her life.

Soft Neurological Signs.
Signs associated with deficits in complex behaviors that are considered possible indicators of brain damage.

Special Ability Tests.
Tests used to measure unique skills.

Specific Language Disability.
A term applied to children with average intelligence who have difficulty in learning to read, write, spell, or communicate in some modality.

Specific Learning Disability.
A term applied to children of average intelligence who have below-average achievement in a particular academic area.

Speed Test.
A test that compares individuals based on speed of performance at some task.

Standard Deviation (SD).
A measure of the spread of scores in a particular group. Computation of the SD is based on the deviation of each individual score from the mean.

Standard Error of Measurement.
An estimate of the error in an individual's score due to the imperfect reliability of a test or measurement procedure.

Standardization.
The process of administering a carefully constructed test to a large, representative sample of people in a standard manner for the purpose of determining norms.

Standardization Sample.
A group consisting of individuals who have been given a test under standard conditions.

Standard Scores.
Scores that represent an individual's distance from the mean in terms of the standard deviation of the distribution.

Standardized Test.
A test that has clear directions for use, adequately determined norms, and reliability and validity data.

Stanine.
A standard score scale with a range of scores from one through nine with a mean of five and a standard deviation of two.

Subtest.
A portion of a test designed to measure a particular aspect of the characteristic or skill that the test as a whole measures.

Test Anxiety.
A feeling of fear that an individual will not do well experienced as the time for testing approaches.

Test Battery.
A collection of tests assembled to gather information for evaluating an individual along a wide spectrum.

Thought Disorder.
A thinking process characterized by illogical or autistic reasoning.

Underachievement.
Performance poorer than that predicted based on aptitude or achievement testing.

Validity.
The degree to which a test actually measures what it claims to measure.

Verbal Test.
A test that requires the use of words as the means for determining ability.

Visual Motor.
A phrase that refers to the coordination of visual input with motor ability.

Word Attack Skills.
The ability to analyze unfamiliar words by syllables and phonemic elements in order to pronounce it.

Annotated Bibliography

The following bibliography is a description of materials related to psychological *testing* alone. There are many books currently in print that help parents to understand and deal with specific disorders, such as Attention Deficit Disorders or Learning-Disabled Children. The present bibliography does not focus on those books. Rather, we have listed only books that are related to the field of psychological testing and assessment.

American Psychological Association. 1981. *American Psychologist*. Testing: Concepts, policy, practice, and research. 36 (October): 10.

A volume of a professional psychological journal devoted solely to the current technical and conceptual issues and problems in psychological testing.

American Psychological Association, American Educational Research Association, and the National Council on Measurement in Education. 1985. *Standards for Educational and Psychological Testing.*

Ethical and professional guidelines adopted by the professional organizations to regulate the development and use of psychological testing.

Anastasi, A. 1988. *Psychological Testing*. 6th ed. New York: Macmillan.

Primarily an undergraduate textbook focusing on test construction, principles of testing, and current testing practices. Includes a list of test publishers, and a classified list of some 240 representative tests.

Barker, P. 1990. *Clinical Interviews with Children and Adolescents*. New York: W. W. Norton & Co.

A book for students describing the variety of interviewing techniques useful with children from infancy through adolescence. The structure and stages of interviewing are discussed, along with a chapter on interviewing mentally retarded children.

Children's Defense Fund. 1978. *Your Child's School Records: Questions and Answers about a Set of Rights for Parents and Students*. Washington, DC.

A booklet put out by an advocacy organization that answers questions parents ask about school records. It also contains the names and addresses of advocacy groups for legal assistance and the addresses of state departments of education.

Children's Defense Fund. 1989. *PL 94-142 and 504: Numbers That Add Up to Educational Rights for Children with Disabilities*. 3rd ed. Washington, DC.

A guide for parents and advocates that answers questions about the special education and civil rights laws and lists state and local advocacy groups, national disability associations, national and regional offices of federal agencies, and state special education departments. Legal references.

The Exceptional Parent (Magazine). P.O. Box 300, Dept. EP, Denville, New Jersey 07834 (telephone: 800-247-8080).

A journal written by professionals intended for parents who have disabled children to assist them in practical matters of daily life and education.

Galvin, M. 1987. *Ignatius Finds Help*. New York: Magination Press.

Designed for children and their parents to be read separately or together to allay anxiety about seeing a psychotherapist. Story is of a bear who has troubles getting along with others.

Joint Committee on Testing Practices. 1988. *Code of Fair Testing Practices in Education*. Available from the American Psychological Association, 1200 Seventeenth Street, NW, Washington, DC 20036.

Major obligations to test takers of professionals who develop and/or use educational tests. Directed primarily at professionally developed tests.

Koocher, B. P., and Keith-Spiegel, P. C. 1990. *Children, Ethics, and the Law*. Lincoln, Nebraska: University of Nebraska Press.

A volume intended for professionals who are concerned about the appropriate practice in the specialized psychological work with children and their families. Deals with issues such as confidentiality, informed consent, and children's rights.

Nemeroff, M. A., and Annuziata, J. 1990. *The First Book of Child Therapy*. Washington, DC: American Psychological Association.

Intended for children ages four through seven to introduce them to play therapy, aimed at answering common questions children and parents have regarding therapy process.

Salvia, J., and Ysseldyke, J. 1991. *Assessment*. Boston: Houghton, Mifflin Co.

A comprehensive introductory level textbook on assessment practices in special and remedial education.

Sattler, J. M. 1988. *Assessment of Children*. 3rd ed. San Diego, California: Jerome M. Sattler Publisher.

A comprehensive widely used graduate-school-level textbook on the psychological assessment of children.

Wodrich, D. L., and Kush, S. 1990. *Children's Psychological Testing: A Guide for Nonpsychologists*. 2nd ed. Baltimore, Maryland: Paul H. Brooks Publishing Company.

Intended for nonpsychologist professionals, it describes various psychological tests used for children of different ages and discusses general diagnostic issues and ways of judging test findings.

In addition to the resources listed above, which are primarily about psychological testing, all states publish information about testing and the rights of parents in the special education process as well, as mandated by PL 94-142. Contact your state board of education to find out what information they provide to parents.

Index